BUSINESS PERFORMANCE IN THE RETAIL SECTOR

The Experience of the John Lewis Partnership

Business Performance in the Retail Sector

Retail Sector

The Experience of the John Lewis Partnership

KEITH BRADLEY
and
SIMON TAYLOR

CLARENDON PRESS · OXFORD
1992

Oxford University Press, Walton Street, Oxford OX2 6DP

Oxford New York Toronto
Delhi Bombay Calcutta Madras Karachi
Petaling Jaya Singapore Hong Kong Tokyo
Nairobi Dar es Salaam Cape Town
Melbourne Auckland

and associated companies in
Berlin Ibadan

Oxford is a trade mark of Oxford University Press

Published in the United States
by Oxford University Press, New York

British Library Cataloguing in Publication Data
data available

Library of Congress Cataloging in Publication Data
Bradley, Keith
Business performance in the retail sector: the experience of the John Lewis Partnership/by Keith
Bradley and Simon Taylor.
Includes bibliographical references and index.
1. John Lewis Partnership—History.   2. Retail trade—Great Britain—Case studies.
3. Profit-sharing—Great Britain—Case studies.   I. Taylor, Simon. II. Title.
HF5429.6.G7B68   1992   381'.45'0006041—dc20   91–32181
ISBN 0–19–825694–9

Typeset by Butler & Tanner Ltd
Frome and London
Printed in Great Britain by
Bookcraft Ltd,
Midsomer Norton
Avon

Preface

This book represents the latest publication of research undertaken by the Business Performance Group. The Business Performance Group was founded in 1985 by Keith Bradley of the London School of Economics staff, with the broad goal of pursuing research relevant to managers in their efforts to improve the performance of business enterprises. In the past, most academics have deliberately kept their distance from commercial enterprises, lest their objectivity be threatened, and have made little effort to explain the relevance of their work to practising managers. A fundamental assumption of the Business Performance Group, in contrast, has been that academics need to develop closer, more collaborative relationships with the business community. In the same spirit of breaking down boundaries, the Business Performance Group has pursued an interdisciplinary, international approach.

This is founded on a belief that when academics set the research agenda with an eye to managerial concerns, their work is more likely to be relevant and useful. Moreover, truly outstanding research often requires detailed data of a kind that businesses will not provide except in the context of a close working relationship. Far from necessitating a compromise in quality, joint ventures with business allow academics to undertake research of a scope and depth that would not otherwise be feasible. Working with top management on issues of mutual concern is likely to be particularly productive in this regard.

Over the past six years, the Business Performance Group has built a reputation as an international centre of excellence in management research and education. Members of the Group have established strong relationships with leaders of the business and policy communities, and have developed a distinctive interdisciplinary approach to understanding management issues. As Professor Michael Porter of the Harvard Business School has observed, the Business Performance Group's work helps to 'unscramble the way we measure and explain performance where the complexity of actual competition is recognized'. Michael Heseltine praised the Group for 'wielding a formidable axe in cutting away the props of a divided society' to reveal the value of co-operation among industry, government and academia.

Research undertaken by members of the Business Performance Group covers a wide spectrum. Recent projects include a study of the relationships between forms of remuneration and individual effort; an examination of mentoring relationships as a means of fostering employee development in a division of Motorola; a study of compensation policy, organization structures, and their effect on corporate performance; a survey of research activities at securities firms in the City; and a broad review of innovative human resource policies at a fast-growing high-tech company.

Keith Bradley has published widely on management, industrial policy, and employee relations. His books include *Worker Capitalism* (quoted as 'one of the most outstanding academic books in the field of management, business and labor relations'), *Cooperation at Work, Share Ownership for Employees*, and *Managing Owners*. He has contributed to *The Economist*, the *Financial Times*, *The Guardian*, and journals ranging from the *Harvard Business Review* to the *Review of Economic Studies*. A consultant to a variety of business, government, and international organizations, Keith Bradley has been a visiting professor at Harvard Business School and the University of Pennsylvania, a fellow of the Harvard Center for Business and Government, and a member of the Multinational Research Advisory Group of the Wharton School.

Simon Taylor is a fellow of St Catharine's College, Cambridge, sometime consultant to the World Bank, and former project director with the Business Performance Group. During his tenure in the Group he was responsible for managing major research projects and contributing to Business Performance Group lectures and seminars and representing the Group in a number of press and current affairs programmes. He is currently working as an analyst in the City. After gaining a first-class honours degree in economics at Cambridge and winning the Wrenbury Scholarship, he undertook graduate research work at Oxford University and the London School of Economics where he gained his Ph.D. For two years he was an Overseas Development Institute Fellow at the Central Bank of Lesotho. His publications include *Research Quality in the City* and *Enhancing Competition: The British Telecom–Mercury Duopoly* (from the Business Performance Group *Papers on Performance* series).

The authors would like to thank Nancy Jackson for her invaluable assistance and advice throughout the development of this book.

Contents

List of Figures

List of Tables

1

Introduction

The need to manage employees as an asset, not a cost, is becoming a prominent theme of management thinking. In many industries the basis of competition is shifting away from economies of scale, towards flexibility and rapid response to changing market requirements. These capabilities may be enhanced by technology, but they rest fundamentally on the efforts of employees who commit their best energies to corporate endeavours.

Recognizing the value of increasing workers' involvement, companies have experimented with a variety of programmes, such as profit-related pay, employee share ownership, and quality circles, over the last two decades. Many of these initiatives have been consciously modelled on the practices of Japanese companies. Japan has no monopoly on effective human resource management, however, nor is enlightened thinking in the West restricted to high-tech industries and advanced manufacturing environments. The John Lewis Partnership, an employee-owned British retail chain, exemplifies a human resource strategy that could well be applied in other sectors. As this book will show, the distinctive John Lewis Partnership approach has been associated with considerable commercial success, as well as unusual stability in the workforce, in an industry where turnover is typically very high.

The idea that people are crucial to the effective running of a commercial organization is nothing new: far-sighted employers in the early nineteenth century identified the gains that could be realized by taking their employees seriously. These include Owen's experiments at New Lanark and the successful paternalistic companies of Cadbury and Rowntree. As organizations grew larger during the early twentieth century, becoming multi-divisional and bureaucratic, they needed to keep track of an ever-larger number of employees. This need gave rise to the personnel function, typically constituted as a separate department of the company, which handled employee information and compensation systems.

In the 1970s and early 1980s, under the spur of intensified international competition, many British firms undertook efforts to improve their productivity, and subsequently their innovation and flexibility. The Japanese example indicated the importance of not only investing in fixed capital, but making full use of the skills and commitment of the workforce. This notion became cofidied in the idea of human resource management. Thinking about employees as human resources focused attention on the potential for gains that had been overlooked under earlier management methods. It became clear that there might be opportunities to employ human assets—a pool of talent and ability—with greater efficiency, and in a manner that would yield greater innovation. The creation of a separate specialized personnel function had diverted attention from what should have been a mainstream management job: exploring and enhancing employees' contributions to long-term profit potential. The recognition of this gap was of considerable practical importance.

Yet, a decade after human resource management began to percolate into mainstream management consciousness, much remains to be done to integrate the organization's human capital with its physical and financial capital. Too often, the only real change has been one of labelling: the former *personnel* department is now called *human resources*. Just as a so-called major initiative on quality may lead to nothing more than a video from the chairman exhorting workers to strive for zero defects, the new human resource management has failed to realize its full potential. There is a danger that human resource management will come to be seen as just one more fad. Organizations have been subjected to a series of managerial 'flavours of the month'—human factors, job enrichment, quality service, just-in-time, and computer-aided manufacturing, to name a few. Each has left a residue of changed practice, but none has really delivered the gains in productivity that it promised. To consign human resource management to this dust-heap would be a tragic mistake. In the future the human side of the business is likely to become more important rather than less. Demographic pressures will make it harder for companies to secure the workforce they need; growing international competition is already exacerbating this problem. Flexibility, employee commitment, and adaptability are becoming ever more crucial. Managing change is the issue of the day, and this task is quintessentially about people.

A major problem in trying to develop a more effective and consistent approach to managing human capital is that these issues have been largely ignored in the analytical frameworks typically used to study the firm's external competitive environment and its optimal financial and production strategies. Over the last few decades, management has made good use of a structured and directed methodology for examining a range of central business questions: is the firm correctly positioned relative to the product market? Is the firm's financial structure optimal? Is the business portfolio properly balanced? Is the internal configuration of productive equipment the most efficient for the output demands? Such analyses, however, seldom pay much attention to the human side of the business. Awkward soft issues, such as change, employee motivation, organizational culture, career development, recruitment, and training, tend to disappear into a large black hole. If these people issues are addressed at all, it is typically with the goal of ensuring conformity with decisions already taken on new production arrangements, a shift in business focus, or a new financial strategy. Personnel management is regarded as the purview of a specialized group of managers, often of no great prestige in the firm.

The John Lewis Partnership, which emerged from a family-owned retail business established in 1864, has taken a very different view of human resource management. In 1929 the heir to the original business, John Spedan Lewis, put the companys' assets into a trust for the benefit of past, current, and prospective employees. His motivations, as discussed in later chapters, may have been largely idealistic, but he also believed the business itself would benefit from the shift in ownership. Twenty-one years later, full voting power was transferred to the trustees in the Partnership.

From the beginning, John Lewis Partnership employees have been regarded as an important asset, rather than a cost, and it has been recognized that personnel policies cannot be separated from basic business or financial strategies. The John Lewis Partnership has steadily expanded to become a very large firm. By the end of the financial year 1989–90 it had a turnover of over £1.8 billion, with a trading profit of around £124 million, and about 30,000 partners. It is thus the largest and one of the longest surviving employee-owned firms in the Western world.

This book investigates how John Lewis's unique ownership and organizational arrangements have influenced the company's commercial performance. Our major finding is that these arrangements, combined with a heightened awareness of the role of people, have given the John Lewis Partnership significant advantages in the market-place. It is well positioned for a future in which firms will be competing more actively for people and skills.

Some 20 years ago competitive advantage in the retail sector was gained through a combination of pricing, technology, and sites. Today, these factors have become far less important as sources of differentiation. It is not clear, for example, that cheaper products or services translate into increased sales. Customers appear to be more discerning and in many cases willing to pay more for what is perceived as better quality. (Witness, for example, the demand in the 1980s for Perrier water and 501 Levi jeans.) With regard to technology, most large retailers have already invested in electronic point-of-sale systems which speed up transactions and provide companies with detailed information on customers and their preferences. A few battles may still be fought at the periphery, but the major investments have been made, gremlins have been removed from systems, and there is less competitive advantage to be gained through further major investments in technology. Similarly, site acquisition is unlikely to offer opportunities for disrupting the competitive equilibrium. The few highly advantaged sites remaining in Britain are extremely costly, and not to be obtained without protracted negotiations.

How then do high street stores create and sustain their competitive advantage? Increasingly, by means of human resource strategies that enable them to deliver excellent customer service. Most large and successful high street stores employ large numbers of people. In the past, because a pool of qualified employees was readily available, it was not necessary to invest in sophisticated personnel strategies. Today the picture is changing, because of increased competition, demographic changes, and skill shortages.

Without an able and committed workforce, no retailer—indeed no company—can hope to meet the rising expectations created by intensified competition. Already standards of product quality, design, and reliability have been driven up, and companies are competing on the basis of flexibility, rapid response to changing market needs, and superior customer service. Excellence in these areas comes from well-motivated and creative employees. Even as the bases of competitive advantage shift, a new organization model is emerging that de-emphasizes conflict and the separation of capital and labour and assigns substantial responsibility to self-governing teams of employees who increasingly own equity in their company. Well suited to the new realities of competition, this model succeeds by tapping the strengths of the workforce. Yet demographic changes will make it harder for companies to attract and retain flexible and skilled labour in the years to come.

These trends pose crucial questions for companies in the future. Managers must work to understand how people contribute to competitive success in their particular business. On that basis, they must then design, implement, and evaluate effective human resource strategies. In addressing these challenges, they will find it useful to consider the practices of other firms, with an eye to identifying the most successful approaches. Increasingly, retail managers are looking to the experience of the John Lewis Partnership for lessons in how to manage people and to develop a committed and well-motivated workforce.

This book focuses on the commercial behaviour and success of the John Lewis Partnership, which distributes its entire profits (after retentions for investment) to its employees, in the form of a bonus. The Partnership is run according to a set of principles laid down by John Spedan Lewis, which provide for a high degree of accountability and representation for all employees and extensive diffusion of information about the firm's activities through a range of in-house journalism. Employee motivation is closely related to the structure of pay: a relationship that is central to developing and sustaining a competitive strategy based on people. As the John Lewis Partnership has found, appropriate compensation arrangements can harness the commitment and creativity of employees, and make it easier to attract desirable new recruits.

We believe that many companies are ready to recognize the lessons implicit in the John Lewis Partnership experience, which apply well beyond the bounds of the retail sector. The future promises to bring important changes in the ways organizations reward their members. In every sector, firms that do not keep up with evolving standards of best compensation practice risk being out performed and out-hired by more forward looking competitors.

Pay and Ownership: Innovation in the 1980s

The 1980s saw a growing interest in new forms of ownership and remuneration for employees, reflecting changes in both the overall context of employee relations and the competitive environment. These trends stimulated companies to innovate, and governments to offer tax advantages to certain types of new institutional arrangements. There was also a growing interest in more participatory management styles that encourage greater commitment and enterprise from the workforce.

There have been two periods of sharp growth in the number of employee share schemes in Britain, both stimulated by changes in tax legislation. The Finance Act of 1972 marked the first period. It accorded tax advantages to certain executive share options and share incentives schemes and to share-based profit-sharing schemes. The Finance Act of 1973 offered favourable tax treatment to Save as You Earn contracts, a new type of scheme which extended shareholding to non-executive employees. The second period of sharp growth started with the Finance Act of 1978 and is still continuing.

At present there are two main groups of employee share schemes which derive tax advantage: approved all-employee share schemes introduced in the Finance Act of 1980 and approved discretionary share option schemes introduced in the Finance Act of 1978. Although there have been many experiments in profit-sharing, employee ownership, and full worker control throughout the twentieth century, new schemes for paying employees increased substantially during the last two decades (Smith 1986). As of 1986, 21 per cent of all firms in Britain used one or more of the various types of all-employee schemes, with a higher level of penetration among publicly quoted companies (Poole 1989: 46).

A closely related phenomenon has been the increase in employee ownership. In the United States, preferential tax treatment has encouraged the growth of Employee Stock Ownership Plans (ESOPs) since the mid-1970s (Rosen, Klein, and Young 1986). Some 8 million workers were involved in ESOPs by the mid-1980s (Poole 1989). In the United Kingdom, ESOPs have only appeared more recently, boosted through the denationalization of state assets. The best-known case is the National Freight Consortium, which combined an employee buy-out with privatization of the National Freight Company (Bradley and Nejad 1989). In 1989, the National Freight Company was floated on the London Stock Exchange with considerable success. It remains distinctive in that shares held by employees carry two votes, compared with one vote for outside shareholders. These developments reflect changes in the broader business context:

1. the growth of competition, increasingly from middle-income and newly industrializing economies; the Japanese example has been extremely influential;
2. a shift in economic and political ideology towards deregulation and reduced intervention by the state; and
3. demographic and other long-term changes in the labour market, affecting the age and sex structure of the workforce.

The 1980s have been described as the third phase of the development of organizational democracy, characterized by an extension of ownership rights and the growth of management and labour buy-outs (Abell 1985). It has been argued that the introduction of more participatory forms of management and remuneration follows a cycle which reflects changing bargaining power between workers and management: participation emerges as a way of buying off worker dissent, only to be removed subsequently as the bargaining position shifts back again (Ramsey 1977; 1983). However, this thesis held up less well in the 1980s, when a combination of high unemployment and government anti-corporatist ideology to some extent reversed the expectations and power of organized labour that built up in the 1970s (Poole 1989). The main driving force behind the changes in the 1980s was the state itself, which used the tax system to encourage the adoption of new remuneration schemes.

The state's interest in this process has been twofold. At the macroeconomic level, it has been argued that by pushing some risk onto labour, flexible payments systems can ease the economy's response to external shocks and reduce unemployment. The main influence here has been the work of Weitzman (1984; 1986), which suggests that profit-share based payment would help to reduce inflation also. The United Kingdom government's support of profit-related pay appears to be based in large part on an interpretation of Weitzman's ideas. At the microeconomic level, profit-sharing and employee ownership may enhance productivity, build commitment to the organization, and lead to more harmonious industrial relations (Bradley and Gelb 1982). From the firm's point of view, the main immediate benefit may be felt in recruitment, particularly if there is a tax advantage to be distributed. Profit-sharing and employee ownership may also assist in developing a decentralized, participatory management style.

Recent research has cast doubt on the macroeconomic benefits claimed for profit-sharing (Blanchflower and Oswald 1987; Wadhwani and Wall 1988). There is more support for some of the microeconomic benefits of profit-sharing and employee ownership. Bell and Hanson (1989) argue that on a wide range of indicators, companies with profit-sharing performed better than those without. Wadhwani and Wall (1988) found some evidence of productivity associated with employee ownership. Other research has demonstrated a positive association between employee participation and productivity, though there are some ambiguities about causality (Defourney, Estrin, and Jones 1985; Conte and Tennenbaum 1978; Whyte *et al.* 1983).

Case study evidence provides support for the harmonizing of industrial relations associated with employee ownership (Bradley and Nejad 1989). Work done by the Business Performance Group at the London School of Economics on the Baxi Partnership suggests that when workers become owners of the firm, they tend to be more critical of management and to demand greater information of them. This observation suggests that employee owners might be able to replace (and certainly to complement) capital markets as a discipline on management.

Objectives of the Book

This book will shed light on the following issues:

1. How commercially successful can an entirely employee-owned firm be, given that orthodox models of performance stress the role of the capital market in ensuring efficiency?
2. How does an emphasis on the human side of the business contribute to commercial performance?

To achieve these goals, we adopt the following research agenda:

1. an historical analysis of the John Lewis Partnership from the earliest part of the century to the present, using a comparative business perspective wherever possible;
2. an analysis of the economic and accounting perspective on employee-owned firms and the predicted performance of such firms;
3. a comparative study of the John Lewis Partnership relative to its main competitors for the period 1970–89, to test the predictions of the orthodox model; and
4. an analysis of the role of human resources in retailing strategy and competitiveness in the late 1980s, based on in-depth interviews with senior decision-makers in the sector.

Existing research has not determined whether (and how) employee ownership and profit-sharing contribute to commercial success. Social scientific research does not yet have a clear model of the extremely complex processes and structures that make up the operation of the firm. Imperfect and incomplete findings are therefore inevitable. Most prior research on innovations in payment and participation has been cross-sectional in nature. Such studies search for strong findings that show up across large numbers of firms and can be isolated from the many other variables that affect firm behaviour. The cross-sectional approach is limited for two reasons:

1. It can only take account of those factors which can be reduced to a quantitative element.
2. It cannot take account of the complex interaction of variables inside the firm.

This book, in contrast, develops a case study of a single firm. Although our approach cannot achieve the generality of more broadly based statistical work, it offers a deeper insight into the interaction of variables that contribute to commercial performance. The case study analysis is supported by and integrated with a comparative perspective.

The John Lewis Partnership has been the subject of a major research project by Flanders, Pomeranz, and Woodward (1968), which remains the most important and influential study of the United Kingdom's largest employee-owned firm. But their work is mainly concerned with the nature and extent of industrial democracy in the organization and only marginally, if at all, with the Partnership as a business. The present work extends the Flanders *et al.* study by taking the business performance of the Partnership as the central issue to be investigated and explained. The mere fact that the organization has survived for so long is a notable achievement, given that much of the orthodox literature derived from financial and economic thinking would predict otherwise (Jensen and Meckling 1979).

The John Lewis Partnership is based on an explicit set of business principles, which support and guide its management. These principles have not previously been examined and placed in context. This study investigates the role of these Partnership Principles in guiding the John Lewis Partnership as a business.

2

A Research Strategy

Introduction

To understand a business such as the John Lewis Partnership requires a broader methodological approach than that of neo-classical economics. In this chapter we lay out a research strategy that takes into account a wider range of data. We first consider the range of data available in principle to the researcher and then place this data in the context of an ideal research strategy for fully mapping out the complex range of determinants of organizational success. Next we detail the difficulties in practice of obtaining the data. A more modest and tractable approach (the research strategy adopted for this study) is then outlined. Conclusions follow.

Data and Sources

Data relevant to the analysis of business can be categorized along the following dimensions:

1. objective or subjective;
2. quantitative or qualitative (hard versus soft);
3. publicly available or confidential; and
4. individual or aggregate.

Table 2.1 summarizes the type of data that are relevant to the analysis of business performance in terms of these categories. The rough-and-ready terms used here are intended only to give some sense of the comparative position of particular data types. For example, although published company financial and economic data are ostensibly hard and objective, the allocation of costs and the interpretation of figures inevitably reflect in some way the interests of those who control them. The norms of following standard practices and retaining independent auditors are designed to prevent outright fraud and to ensure as much comparability as possible, but some range of choice inevitably remains for the exact presentation of the underlying data.

TABLE 2.1. *Business data types*

Data type	Objective or subjective	Hard or soft	Publicly available or private	Individual or aggregate
1. Company accounts	Objective	Hard	Public	Individual
2. Other company financial and economic data	Objective	Hard	Private	Individual
3. Official (e.g. CBI) data	Objective/ subjective	Hard/soft	Public	Aggregate
4. Employee attitudes	Subjective	Hard/soft	Private	Individual
5. Personal interviews	Subjective	Soft	Private	Individual
6. Observation data	Subjective	Soft	Private	Individual

Table 2.1 includes many more types of data than would typically be used in econometric studies of firm behaviour. It also covers a broader array of data than is normally used in the organizational behaviour literature (which is often concerned with non-market or non-commercial organizations, so that certain types in the table are not applicable).

Published company accounts are a mainstream source of research data. Subject to the qualifications above, they offer a reliable and standardized set of information, particularly on the financial side. In combination with official data on, for example, price indices, they permit the construction of a wide range of conventional performance measures, such as production functions, financial ratios analysis and growth of assets, real sales, and so forth. The data in published company accounts are predominantly financial in nature. Activities that are critical to the business's future growth may show up only as current costs. In particular, the balance sheet does not show the value of human capital in the firm, and such assets as brands and research and development have only recently begun to creep into the analysis. The possibilities for estimating (for example) production functions are limited without a more detailed description of the workforce and of the actual use of the capital stock.

The item 'other company data' includes a range of information that is highly useful for a deeper understanding of performance, although not normally available from public sources. Such items are typically omitted from the accounts because they do not fit easily with the predominantly financial orientation of the framework, although they may be items that are of commercial confidence. However, this is true of nearly all the items in the published accounts and it is inevitably difficult to draw the line between what the directors of the firm would like to keep out of the public domain and what is necessary to communicate to shareholders. The main items of research interest are: the age, skill, and occupational structures of the labour force; hours worked and overtime; capacity utilization and down-time; and expenditure on training and research and development.

Employee attitude data may be essentially subjective, but they can be quantified within useful limits. When quantitative tests are used, their power depends very much on the design of the questionnaire and the circumstances of data collection, including centrally the role of the company management. Attitudinal data are potentially quite *hard*. The use of questionnaire data on personnel can vastly improve the researcher's picture of the company.

The value of fixed assets is largely dependent on their relation in production with the workers who use them. By exploring questions of morale, organization, communication, waste, and maintenance, attitude surveys can permit a much more detailed appraisal of the underlying productivity position. These data also shed light on whether current financial and productivity positions are sustainable, by revealing the extent to which a particular performance has been squeezed out of the workforce by essentially short-term means. Going further, questionnaires can provide a basis for at least a rudimentary balance sheet appraisal of the human capital in the company. This procedure embraces skills, career expectations, levels of enthusiasm, and experience. Such information should also reveal how closely the firm's practice matches the desired pattern of promotions and career development. By auditing the *goodwill* of key staff towards the firm, such an appraisal offers a further check on the sustainability of a particular level of performance.

Aggregate data available from official sources, and from such bodies as the Confederation of British Industry and the National Economic Development Office, are usually objective and quantifiable. Some surveys of business trends, however, include estimates of confidence and capacity working which derive from the correspondents' subjective estimate of the circumstances of their own firms and of the wider economic climate. Many of these trends are quantified in index form, but usually only the direction of the trend, or at best the rough order of magnitude, can be applied with much confidence. Sectoral surveys based on interviews with relevant suppliers or customers may be highly important, as, for example, in assessing the role of quality factors in export performance, but it is intrinsically difficult to obtain such evidence in a directly quantifiable form. Even relatively impressionistic data may be useful for analysis, however.

The more subjective data that are thrown up by the sociological techniques are also more *soft*, in the sense of difficult to quantify. This is almost certainly why they have not been used very much in conventional economic research. In effect, unfortunately, a major source of information about the company's workings has been set aside. Economic theory's tendency to exclude any variables that cannot be rendered easily in mathematical terms leads to the exclusion of information that may be essential to the analysis. Local idiosyncrasies and special circumstances require more data to be interpreted. Economic models give guidance on the broad direction of questioning and offer some stylized results to test against the case study findings. Thereafter, however, the softer data often turn out to be more relevant. This iterative process ought eventually to feed back into the economic models themselves, adjusting the balance of what the theory seeks to explain. There is no need, indeed it is positively damaging, for the two sides of the study to appear in conflict.

The softer data fall into two categories. First, interviews can reveal a great deal of information bearing on the organizational culture and the underlying politics and perceptions of the relationships within the firm. Second, the use of participant observation analysis can usefully supplement the interviews, filling the gaps in understanding that inevitably rise. Direct observation also gives an extra level of insight into many procedures within the firm. The stated function of a particular meeting may in practice be less important than the actual outcome and how that was arrived at. Interviewing, asking, listening, and observing are crucially important, along with casual observation of the physical and geographical structure of the company. Small scraps of anecdotal evidence are often highly useful leads in the interview. An appreciation of subtle oddities about the plant can be of considerable importance. Interviewees may fail to mention some aspect of the firm which is in fact quite peculiar, simply because they regard it as so well established as to need no comment.

The range of data that might be used in a study of business performance is clearly immense, and there has to be some cut-off point. If we work on the principle that performance and company behaviour are fundamentally about human interaction and relationships, then it is in this area of the data that the really important and discriminating bits of information are likely to emerge.

An Ideal Research Programme

By using all of the data sources listed in Table 2.1, the researcher ought to be able to explain business success and failure much better than either conventional economic appraisal or traditional organizational behaviour studies. But no unified research strategy has yet been developed to integrate all of these data in a fully efficient and coherent manner.

Within the organizational literature Reed (1985) attempts a more comprehensive approach, suggesting that there are four important levels of analysis:

1. Cognitive mapping—the explication of the concepts that agents use to make sense of their actions, the framework of assumptions and beliefs.
2. Interpretive understanding—focusing on the relationship between the cognitive maps and the associated social activities.
3. Structural analysis—analysis of the distributional and allocation systems relevant to the agent's practice, and an explication of the power relationships.
4. Historical reconstruction—institutional analysis.

The economic activities and analyses sketched above relate to the first three levels defined by Reed, but especially to the third.

Cognitive mapping and interpretive understanding are to a large extent determined a priori in most economic theory. Economic analysis works from the point of view of a theoretical perfectly rational agent, so there is no inherent conflict with the hermeneutic intent of Reed's second level. In practice, however, the evidence that agents do not necessarily use the cognitive methods attributed to them by economic theory is likely to be problematic.

It is therefore at the third level that economics seems likely to have its greatest influence on organizational thinking. Any discussion of the structural context of organizational behaviour is necessarily concerned with the economic environment. This holds true both for market organizations and for those that deliver goods or services as their main formal goal, even if they are not directly part of the market economy (e.g. hospitals and public agencies).

Even for institutions that have no economic context in this sense (e.g. political parties and pressure groups), much may be gained from an awareness of the economics of organization.

Although Reed provides an interesting and fruitful starting point, it will be a long and evolutionary task to convert his typology of analysis into a fully workable system that can embrace data and approaches from the various relevant disciplines. In the mean time, short-term expedients are necessary, because such a comprehensive range of data is very unlikely to be available.

Problems of Access

The full range of data that could in principle be collected is seldom available. Quite simply, the data collection process imposes costs on the firm that it would prefer to avoid. First there is the financial cost of resources used up, consisting primarily of the time of personnel diverted from other tasks, but also including such ancillary costs as photocopying and telephone calls. Many of these costs are relatively trivial, but they still represent a consumption of shareholder's money, which must not be taken for granted.

Second, the process of conducting research alters relationships in the organization. From the moment that the research team enters the firm, the object of study is changed. Beyond the transient problem of distorting the object by measuring it, the organization may be permanently changed. People have memories: information brought out into the open by the research process may affect the nature of confidences and trust relations between organization members. This is not necessarily a damaging process; indeed it may be positively useful to the firm. If internal communications between departments or persons are poor, the research process may help to pinpoint just where the real data lie and what might be done to improve the process. The third potential cost comes from the risk of disclosing sensitive data. Since the researchers cannot know just what constitutes such data, firms typically impose a blanket ban on revealing any company-specific data without prior and explicit permission. Such a ban would need to be modified in the case of an attributable case study that clearly identified its subject—which involves a much bigger risk for any firm. In many research projects, such permission is granted *ex post*, when the relative costs and benefits to the firm of disclosure are clearer. Published studies of the performance of named commercial institutions are likely to be biased heavily in favour of successful ones; very few chairmen would wish to see a critical study appear publicly.

A fourth potential cost to the firm is the undermining of authority that may result from investigation of working procedures. Anything that reveals or highlights the incompetence of managers or supervisors will cause resentment and obstruction. Such effects may damage the study itself, and could create problems for the senior management, which may have been unaware of the situation or have preferred to turn a blind eye. Once again the object of investigation is being altered. The research team will not be given much support if they are perceived as aiming to trap people and tell the management.

Firms may not be aware of all these potential costs as they evaluate requests for data. But clearly researchers should not count on being able to carry out a comprehensive data collection programme. Practical research strategies need to be less ambitious.

A Practical Research Approach

The research problem presented by our study was how to analyse the commercial behaviour of an unusual type of firm and to explain its relative failure or success. Given the difficulties of obtaining comprehensive data, we have followed a twofold strategy. It was clearly essential to use available economic and financial data to investigate the conventional side of commercial behaviour. In addition, however, we needed a different type of data to go beyond the purely economic.

The John Lewis Partnership remains very much the brainchild of John Spedan Lewis and is founded on a set of ideas and principles which he fashioned into two legal settlements and a constitution (see below). We therefore can derive from Lewis's many writings a theory of business, which is likely to be very close to the working principles of the Partnership. The role of the human side of business emerges from this theory and sets up a benchmark for comparison with the Partnership's competitors in the retail trade.

The analysis proceeds in three stages. The first consists of a business history of the John Lewis Partnership. Whilst its story has previously been told in summary fashion (in, for example, Flanders *et al.*), such accounts have not focused on the Partnership as a business. The historical analysis given here is derived from three sources: the writings of Spedan Lewis; interviews with the existing Chairman, Peter Lewis, and the former Chairman, Sir Bernard Miller; and the accounts of the Partnership going back as far as possible, augmented by unpublished notes and papers made available by the Partnership to the authors. This study gives historical context to the performance of the company and highlights some practical aspects of running an employee-owned business.

The second stage of our research was to use the conventional publicly available accounting data to assess the performance of the John Lewis Partnership as a commercial concern in relation to its competitors. In stage three we use in-depth interviews with key decision-makers in other retail firms to provide a detailed analysis of the role of strategy and the determinants of competitive success in retailing in the late 1980s. This analysis is then used to support a comparison of the roles of human resources in the John Lewis Partnership and in the retail sector as a whole.

Whilst other data, for example, replicating the employee questionnaire survey of Flanders *et al.*, would be invaluable in getting to the heart of the Partnership and comparing it with other firms, something that these authors did not do, this is not at present practicable. A replication of the Flanders *et al.* survey in the John Lewis Partnership alone would not address the research problem in this study, namely the commercial performance of the Partnership relative to its competitors. Our research programme builds on findings from the more conventional economic and financial analysis to motivate a second stage of research using a different type of data and a different methodological approach. The synthesis of

these two investigations forms a powerful research strategy covering a wider range of information. It simultaneously addresses the
difficulties of the narrow conception of behaviour and performance
in the neo-classical economics framework and the relative neglect of
commercial and market-related variables in organizational analysis.

Conclusion

This chapter has discussed the range of data potentially available for
the researcher interested in the human side of business performance.
Each of these types of data is used at various times in different
fields of research, and each is valuable. The failure to use them
together reflects the problem of *addivity* of knowledge in this
area. If all of the data were available, a comprehensive research
framework would be necessary to organize the analysis. One such
proposed framework is that of Reed (1985). However, this remains
a difficult task to complete, chiefly because of the various methodological debates within the social sciences. In practice, moreover,
data availability is seriously constrained, for reasons outlined above.
In consequence, more pragmatic strategies are necessary. Our own
approach to the research problem used three types of data to
provide: an historical analysis; a financial and economic comparative
study based on public accounting data; and a second comparative
study based on in-depth interviews.

3

Strategy, Competitiveness, and the Way Ahead

The requirements for competitive success in the retail sector are changing, with important consequences for company decision-makers. Recent interviews with leading managers in both food and non-food companies suggest that their strategic thinking is currently a mixture of old and new.[1] Sites, technology, and merchandising are still considered important. For the future, however, these exutives suspect that the recruitment, training, and motivation of people will be increasingly critical to success. Advantage will lie in human resources, a development quite new in the retail sector.

Retailing in the Late 1980s

By *competitiveness* in retailing, we mean the ability to sell goods or services at prices and in quantities that permit the firm to make sufficient profit to continue activities over a sustained period. While the time horizon (a sustained period) cannot be precisely defined, one thing is clear: no firm can be sure of future success merely because its current position is strong.

The British retail sector underwent rapid structural change in the 1980s. Substantial financing was available for mergers and take-overs (in some cases followed fairly quickly by demergers). These events both reflected and influenced changes in the determinants of retailing competitiveness. Although the sector has been affected

[1] Interviews for this book were conducted with leading executives and unionists between 1989 and 1990.

by external factors, such as cheaper technology and demographic pressures, much of the pressure for greater competitiveness comes from within retailing itself. All profit-seeking institutions acting in a market environment face the same basic task: producing what the consumer wants to buy, and *getting the product right* at a price that covers cost. These fundamental imperatives have a special flavour in retailing, however. A crucial distinction from industrial firms, with major implications for cost control and economies of scale, is that the retailers' product is a service: they present goods for sale, but do not in general produce them. Productivity is generally harder to raise in the service sector, which has been a constant source of difficulty as upward pressure on wages persists. New technology promises to improve productivity in service functions in the future, but there are limits to what can be achieved.

The elements that determine competitiveness in retailing—technology and systems, warehousing and distribution, sites and location, design and merchandising, personnel and human resources—are important in other sectors as well. What is distinctive to retailing is the balance among these determinants and the relative importance accorded to them. That balance has varied historically, with different elements receiving different emphasis at different times. Our interviews show that the debate still continues. Given the rapid pace of change in recent years, there is a considerable range of opinion on what balance is correct now and for the future.

The elements of retail competitiveness interact in various ways associated with different strategies: in some the technology is central, in others the merchandise, while still others focus on the human element. Differences in opinion almost certainly reflect a great deal of uncertainty about the trends and about the need for investment. Technology is expensive, but a well-trained and committed workforce does not come cheap either, and a new superstore now carries such risk that a single failure could damage the company's long-term future.

The View from the Top

Our interviews with retail decision-makers provide considerable insight into the state of the sector today and the shape of retail strategy tomorrow. We will look at the executives' views on the overall determinants of competitiveness, and then turn to the key dimensions of competition: technology and systems, sites and location, and human resources.

What makes a commercially successful retailer? Sometimes, our interviews suggest, it is a matter of emphasis in an increasingly complex and uncertain world. The nature of the product makes a difference, but quality alone is not generally seen as crucial. Consumers are looking for such factors as quality, accessibility, and service. John Hardman, Chairman of ASDA Group plc, sees the balance in his way: 'Quality and value for money are uppermost. But service is now important. Price is still very important, but higher prices are now acceptable if the quality is right.' Roger Saoul, head of Economic Information at Marks and Spencer plc, attributes this shift largely to greater affluence and discrimination among consumers: 'The customer is now more demanding. In the 1950s there was a shortage of goods. Now there are plenty and also wide choice. The customer can go elsewhere if he wants to or if the size and colour are unavailable.'

Some price sensitivity remains, of course. As Sir Terence Conran, then Chairman of Storehouse plc, put it: 'Anyone who wants to maintain market share has two areas to look at. One is quality and the other price. Quality does play a large part in attracting customers, but it won't do it all. So price then also has to be a factor.' Rarely is competition based entirely on price, however. As David Sainsbury, Deputy Chairman of J. Sainsbury plc, observed: 'The basic price is the same throughout the [food] sector. So the difference is made by customer relations. This boils down to a good checkout, EPOS [electronic point-of-sale systems] that do everything.' Self-service has come to seem 'a bit soulless,' said John Hardman, adding that 'people now want good service, availability and helpfulness.'

Greater competitive pressure within the retail sector has given companies the incentive to invest in making improvements. The entire *rounded package* of retail services, not just the goods themselves, must be competitive. George Willoughby, Deputy Chairman of House of Fraser plc, makes the point: 'One of the reasons we believe we sell so much is that we are perceived to be solid, dependable people. Our overall package, including credit and delivery facilities, is seen to be good.' Sir Simon Hornby, Chairman, W. H. Smith and Son plc, attributes primary importance to space allocation: having the right things on the shelves. Roger Saoul mentions several factors as important to competitiveness, including the accessibility of stores, cost structures, technology ('how we control our costs is a very big part of how we manage the business'), and service.

Three factors are crucial to 'getting the product right' in retailing: technology and systems, sites and locations, and human resources. ('The rest, things like money, you can always get', said David Sainsbury.) Differences in emphasis on these inputs reflect differing approaches to competitive strategy.

Technology and Systems

Technology and systems have emerged as a major aspect of modern retailing. In this respect Britain has lagged behind the United States, perhaps partly because of the relative shortage of retail workers in the United States, Sir Simon Hornby suggests. In any case, reductions in the cost of technology, combined with increasing concentration in the retail sector (especially in foods), have given a new impetus to the development of computer-based systems. By capturing information about what is leaving the shelves each day, such systems permit better stock control and better use of space in the shop; they also speed up check-out productivity and customer throughput. Moreover, they give the retailer valuable information about customers' spending habits, on a daily, weekly, and seasonal basis; information from the use of store credit cards makes it possible to correlate the characteristics of customers and their purchases.

Systems have costs as well as benefits, however. They are

expensive to develop and may be disruptive to install. Some members of the organization may resist the adoption of a new system because it calls for new management and employee policies, and often for retraining. Moreover, mistakes made in the use of new systems may be highly damaging to the reputation of the business; errors and failures may cause customers to go elsewhere.

The timing of investment in technological innovation has been an important issue in retailing. Some of the pioneers, it appears, experienced difficulties with the new technology that allowed their competitors to leap-frog ahead. Retailers who have held back too long, on the other hand, may find it is now too late to catch up.

The development and installation of new technology has important implications for other aspects of the business, such as human resource management and design. Technology strategies in retailing focus primarily on distribution and marketing. The importance of central distribution and warehouse systems has grown tremendously and, according to Sir Terence Conran, has changed the relationship between the retailer/wholesaler and the manufacturer: 'There has been a huge investment by the bigger retailers in property and retail systems: distribution. Before, the manufacturer did all that for you, he delivered the goods to your store. We all now have a vast computerized distribution network which controls from the point-of-sale to the manufacturer.' This side of the technology, though, appears to be taken for granted, possibly because it is an obvious application that mimics systems developed in other business areas, such as optimal inventory control and financial planning. The more innovative aspect of technology, in David Sainsbury's opinion, is its potential for marketing and merchandising:

Information technology is likely to be critical in the future. Use of information used to be very poor, but is now much better and will continue to improve. EPOS matters because of the data that it provides. We can now target profit per square foot quite precisely. We can also tailor individual shops to fit local data and effectively use central distribution. Future profits will depend heavily on the use of data and information technology.

Although food retailers have been leaders in applying information technology, similar systems are expected to prove important in other parts of the sector as well. As Roger Saoul points out, the use of electronic point-of-sale in conjunction with in-store credit cards and charge card offers powerful marketing information:

You have got the names of your most committed customers in a databank. By the time our EPOS systems are fully bedded down, detailed information will be available on every single one of the customers. Then, whenever an individual's card is used we will be able to say, 'just a minute, this man has kids but he doesn't buy the children's clothes. Why? Do we need to improve that segment?' Information is a great marketing tool.

Some observers caution against excessive reliance on technology. As Sir Terence Conran points out, the data available from electronic point-of-sale systems is essentially backward looking; local and forward looking analysis is still required. A typical centrally managed merchandising system, he explains, analyses recorded sales by category over a season and reallocates space in a high street location accordingly. Through such reallocations: 'You gradually squeeze one product to the detriment or benefit of another, without knowing why. You trade for that particular location on the basis of history rather than on a real marketing plan. With communications, flexibility, and the ability to analyse products and what the competition are doing in a particular location, makes a much more dynamic use of your data base.'

A related danger is that the technology will scare off the customer, especially if service appears to deteriorate. Gordon Roddick, Chairman, Body Shop, observed: 'I've seen more scrambled eggs arriving out of EPOS than in anything else. It's a huge problem. You can actually see just how damned angry consumers become waiting for ten minutes as coding goes on, before the prices come out. We tend to go for ease of input rather than anything else.'

Like its competitors, the John Lewis Partnership has implemented electronic point-of-sale systems. given its relatively centralized management system and long-standing central buying operation, the Partnership should realize benefits of information technology at least as great as those achieved by other firms. The importance of avoiding a conflict with customer service would be even greater in the Partnership case.

Sites and Locations

The competitive importance of sites and locations in retailing represents a significant difference from industrial firms. For retailers, the prime sites (whose nature may have altered over time) are crucial, and inherently limited in number. Access and a large catchment area—long recognized as essential for high-volume shops such as supermarkets—have become even more important with the emergence of very large shops (superstores) that reap economies of scale and permit a wide range of merchandise. New large sites can also take advantage of the improvements in distribution made possible by the new computer systems. The supply of suitable sites is uncertain, however, since it depends partly on political factors at both national and local levels. In addition, it may be more difficult to recruit personnel for out-of-town developments.

Within towns, in traditional shopping areas, these are different issues. Access may still be important, but factors like ambience and architecture are becoming increasingly relevant. The strategic importance of environmental concern goes beyond attracting customers to use one shopping area rather than another; the recent annual reports of major retailers such as Tesco plc, J. Sainsbury plc, and the John Lewis Partnership have emphasized the environmentally conscious side of their new developments as a matter of public relations in a broad sense.

The central importance of sites is accepted generally. As John Hardman said: 'Sites are important. Site development is critical. Any opportunity must be taken to raise the value added in the shop: its accessibliity and visibility.' Richard Weir, Director, the Retail Consortium, likewise, emphasized that: 'Location, sites, getting the right shops in the right places, probably was always the most important thing. If anything it has grown in importance.

The principal competition between the largest retailers is getting themselves located, in the right place: whether they can provide the right facilities for the right people.' In a sense, he suggested, retailing is a subset of the leisure industry; thus stores must compete with leisure centres and theme parks.

Although critical to competitive success, the site is not entirely within the retailer's control. Important roles are played by investment from the public sector and planning decisions that affect transport and access. A retailer trying to decide between two alternative sites faces the risk that forces beyond its control will change the relative economics. Richard Weir explains: 'Even within the high street itself, changes [which are] taking place very much depend on a number of factors. These include transport, facilities generally available, a relocation of, for example, a bus station—these can radically alter the attraction of one end of the high street from another.'

The choice between owning and renting a site is also important. As Roger Saoul points out, leases give flexibility and short-term liquidity, but at the cost of longer-term uncertainty:

Quite apart from those physical and commercial changes, you get the reality that leases end, retailers aren't always able to accept the rent reviews and so you get changes of location among even major retailers. There are very few retailers today who own a significant number of freeholds and even where they do, those were acquired many years ago on premises that are almost certainly too small.

A major issue in site selection during the late 1980s has been the relative merits of out-of-town developments versus existing city centre locations. Because lack of space and problems of rural development in green belt zones have severely restricted the growth of out-of-town sites in the United Kingdom, there has been a corresponding renewal of interest in improving the city centre facilities. Richard Weir observes: 'Many people will have noticed, for example, a deterioration in Bond Street, associated in part with the deterioriation of Oxford Street. To some extent this has been reversed by very heavy investment on the part of the major retailers. That sort of pattern can be seen all over the country.' He expects to see a few, but not many, more out-of-town shopping centres developed. Similarly, while he acknowledges the import- ance of out-of-town sites, Roger Saoul adds: 'We don't envisage shifting the whole of our real estate from the high street to out of town. We see the need for a complementary offer which will support the inner city offer.

Good sites are in short supply, limiting retailers' ability to exploit economies of scale and forcing new types of development. Looking ahead, says Saoul: 'I think the availability of suitable sites is going to be critical. A suitable site for [the company] today is 40,000 square feet in a square shape. And they don't exist. For that reason, we have taken a number of steps which include the development of satellites selling just one range of goods.

The wholesale development of out-of-town sites would en- counter considerable opposition in any case. As Garfield Davies, General Secretary of the Union of Shop, Distributive and Allied Workers, (USDAW) points out, some groups tend to suffer from the change in location and access, including possibly the staff:

There isn't enough consideration given to how planning appli- cations and the development of large out-of-town shopping pre- cincts can destroy traditional centre city shopping. Insufficient attention is given to infrastructure, particularly transportation. Not enough attention is paid to people who are unable to go to these out-of-town centres: the elderly, the people without transport. Not only are these people unable to go there, but they find that because of the decline of traditional centre city shopping areas, their choice is diminished. Further, how do you get shop workers to and from these out of town sites. If they are working late, what are the dangers involved for them?

The John Lewis Partnership has steered a middle course in site selection. During fifty years of expansion, it took care to obtain good sites that offered potential for growth. Many of its recent new stores are located in existing high streets. Questions of access and transport for staff in remote developments would tend to be larger issues for the Partnership than for conventionally organized retailers, since John Lewis owner-employees could be expected to raise such grievances at the outset. This difference does not necessarily mean a competitive disadvantage, however, since it may be more helpful to acknowledge such problems at the start rather than only after the investment has been made.

Human resources

The leading British retailers interviewed for this study emphasized importance of sites and technology. Yet there are limited opportunities to achieve sustainable advantage in these areas. Sites are increasingly difficult to get, and the technology can be readily purchased as more and more expertise becomes available, especially from the United States. At the margin, accordingly, competition is likely to centre on people, both high-quality management and flexible staff who give good service. Our major focus in this book will be on the human resource side of retailing competitiveness. In particular, we will explore whether its distinctive organizational structure has proven to be an advantage to the John Lewis Partnership.

Except in a handful of firms, retail employees have not historically been given much opportunity to demonstrate their potential. Now, however, there is a new focus on service and on the interface between customer and staff. To some extent this shift reflects the fact that leading retail competitors have achieved virtual parity on other dimensions of competition; at the same time it is consistent with trends in other industries to regard customer service as the root of competitive advantage. The new customer emphasis makes heavy demands on the recruitment, training and motivation systems, and techniques used by retailers.

A second important human resource consideration in retailing is the quality of decision-making. The organization of the larger, more integrated retailing concerns demands a skilled and professional management team—a considerable challenge in a sector that has not traditionally been a popular choice for graduate labour.

Our interviews with executives confirm this sense that people will be central to future competitive success in retailing. Anita Roddick, Managing Director of Body Shop, states the point well:

'You can have a superb warehouse, you can have all the EPOS, you can have computers, and then the customer walks into the shop and a member of staff says, 'I don't know, it's over there.' And the customer says, 'Oh Christ, I'm off.' Where's your sale? Everything begins and ends at the point where the customer meets the sales-person.' The sector has been weak on service in the past, Gordon Roddick observed: 'One of the things that happens in retailing is that nobody is caring about the customer, nobody is taking the time to say, "Here is this new customer who is incredibly mobile and wants instant information".'

Belatedly, the importance of the human dimension is now being recognized. Sir Terence Conran drew attention to its impact on staff retention: 'We've been through the design thing, we're half way through the technology thing. What about people? The service thing is what none of us has really managed. You live in a retail world where 50 per cent of your staff leave you in a year.' If human resource management will indeed be critical to future success in retailing, other firms may have something to learn from the John Lewis experience, for its entire business philosophy orients the Partnership towards an emphasis on employee and personnel issues.

4

A Business History of the John Lewis Partnership

From Inception to the First Act of Settlement

Three features make the John Lewis Partnership interesting from the perspective of management and organizational behaviour:

1. It has been owned by its employees through a trust since 1929.
2. Its employees, or *partners*, receive all of the firm's profits, after retentions, in the form of a partnership bonus.
3. The firm is organized around a constitution that specifies a particular form of employee participation, including the power (in well-defined circumstances) to remove the incumbent chairman.

Although much of the traditional literature suggests that employee ownership and profit-sharing are not compatible with commercial viability, the John Lewis Partnership has survived and grown throughout this century and has a strong reputation amongst customers and competitors. Its experience suggests that some degree of power can be shared with employees without jeopardizing commercial decision-making.

This chapter and the next draw extensively on John Spedan Lewis's account of the firm's early years in his book *Partnership For All* (Lewis 1954), supplemented by the authors' interviews with the current Chairman of the Partnership, Peter Lewis, and his predecessor, Sir Bernard Miller.

The Early Development of the John Lewis Partnership

Background: John Lewis senior

John Spedan Lewis entered a business that had been established by his father in 1864. (See Table 4.1 for a chronology of major events in the firm's history.) In the hands of John Lewis senior, the business was essentially sound and profitable overall, but riddled with inefficiencies, in his son's view. The main problem, thought Spedan Lewis, was his father's obsession with holding wages to the lowest level he could get away with; the result was poor quality labour and a lack of commitment to the firm (Lewis, 1954: 10).

Despite an eccentric tendency to spend large amounts of money on ultimately hopeless legal cases, John Lewis senior maintained a

TABLE 4.1. *John Lewis Partnership: chronology of main events*

Date	Main event
1864	John Lewis senior sets up Oxford Street store.
1912	First Committee for Communication is set up at Peter Jones.
1914	Spedan Lewis acquires Peter Jones from father.
1920	First distribution of Partnership benefit is made at Peter Jones, equivalent to seven weeks' pay.
1928	Death of John Lewis leaves Spedan Lewis as sole owner of the Oxford Street store.
1928	John Lewis and Company is made a public company; acquires T. J. Harries store.
1929	Irrevocable settlement in trust for benefit of current and prospective partners of Lewis and Jones; Trust acquires all voting shares for £1 million in form of interest-free loan from Spedan Lewis, who retains voting power as Chairman of Trust.
1940	Acquisition of 15 stores from Selfridge Provincial brings total to 18 stores and 33 food shops with total employment of 11,000 partners.
1950	Partnership completed with transfer of full voting power in John Lewis Partnership Ltd to trustees.
1955	Spedan Lewis resigns as Chairman; Bernard Miller takes over.
1970	All bonuses now and henceforth paid in cash, rather than securities.
1989	Capital employed £594 million; turnover £1,918 million; membership 37,900.

restrictive attitude to money that his son attributed to his early experience of poverty. This 'delight in thrift' was nonetheless allied to 'a temperament [that] was strongly towards equality and freedom', and which happily endorsed the prospect of Spedan and his brother going to university.

Apart from his views on wages, moreover, John Lewis maintained principles which appeared to work very effectively in business: 'From first to last, ... my father held steadily to a simple policy of genuine solid service. He took immense pains to have constantly in stock the greatest possible choice in goods of certain kinds. He took equal pains to give really good value and to win in all other ways a first-rate reputation for general trustworthiness' (Lewis 1954: 15). But Spedan Lewis concluded that his father's attitude to the staff's pay had prevented John Lewis Limited from realizing its full potential. He describes his father as having 'achieved a great but not a really first-class success by the exertion of great gifts in an occupation that was really far from being his natural field' (Lewis 1954: 12). This success he rated as somewhat lower than that of the contemporaries Owen Owen and William Whiteley, for example.

Nontheless, the firm was worth some £300,000 in the early twentieth century, providing Spedan and his brother, as partners, around £26,000 per year in interest and profit. This sum was about the same as the total wage bill. Considerations of efficiency as well as equity seemed to argue for change, Spedan Lewis came to believe. The main inefficiency in the firm seemed to stem from the unattractive package of pay and benefits offered to employees (pensions and sick pay were minimal, for example). Therefore, Spedan Lewis argued, matters could be improved by distributing to the partners only the interest on their 5 per cent stock, and using the profits to fund better remuneration for the workers.

The Peter Jones Experiment

Spedan Lewis had little success in persuading his father to try out his ideas about pay and profit sharing at John Lewis Limited. His first opportunity came with the Chelsea store Peter Jones acquired in 1906 on the death of its founder. Results from this store were so disappointing that John Lewis senior gave Spedan a free hand to run it, so long as he did so outside the hours he worked for the main shop in Oxford Street. In 1914 Spedan was given the full equity ownership in Peter Jones (conceding his one-quarter ownership in the main store), and was able to begin his experiment.

An initial difficulty was how to raise pay when there was as yet no surplus to distribute. The idea that solved this problem came to Spedan Lewis while he was recuperating in hospital after a riding accident in 1910. Instead of cash, he realized, he could distribute non-voting stock to employees, thereby protecting the decision rights of existing owners and the liquidity of the firm. This distribution of stock was to be the main vehicle of recovery in the store, but many other important changes were also made. Peter Jones began to recruit professional people with no expertise in retailing, including a former Treasury civil servant who later became chief financial adviser to the Partnership. This liberal recruitment policy, distinctive for the retailer sector, has been pursued ever since by the John Lewis Partnership.

In 1912 Spedan Lewis set up the first Committees for Communication between rank-and-file workers and the principal management. The diffusion of information that became a hallmark of the John Lewis Partnership began with the disclosure of trading figures to all employees in the firm, on a departmental basis—a startling departure from traditional ways of doing business in retailing. The trading figures were accompanied by 'a commentary that was intended to have some dynamic value' (Lewis 1954: 38). So far as was possible, pay was increased for all staff. It was difficult to get the first committee off the ground, Lewis records; in fact, it folded after a few weeks and had to be actively resuscitated. This initial apathy is scarcely surprising, if only because few of the workers could have recognized the grand plan in Lewis's mind. The committee (and later the Partnership benefit) must have seemed like a welcome but largely incomprehensible development, the work of a benevolent eccentric, dabbling enthusiastically in social engineering.

Peter Jones's financial position rose from a loss of £8,000 in

1914 to a profit of £20,000 in 1920, the year of the first Partnership benefit. These results were almost certainly inflated by the general profitability of wartime trading. In any case, the improvement in performance was not due directly to the new Partnership benefit, but rather to a general improvement in management and in the climate of work. Spedan Lewis's recollections give some hint of the atmosphere at the time: 'I was seeking to start a community that by this time, I was, I think, already conscious would resemble in some respects the Religious Orders of the Middle Ages' (Lewis 1954: 29). The Partnership benefit (Lewis specifically preferred this term to *profit-sharing*) was first paid in share promises, rather than cash, on the grounds that this arrangement was less likely to attract unfavourable attention from John Lewis. The share promises were to be converted into negotiable stock at some later date. Special requests for conversion into cash were accepted, mostly in cases of people leaving the firm. In 1923, John Lewis senior noted with approval the commercial success of the Peter Jones store, and Spedan Lewis was acepted back as a one-quarter share partner in the main firm.

The development of the Partnership system was also influenced by a post-war strike at the John Lewis Oxford Street store, motivated by the staff's resentment at not sharing in the inflated wartime profits. The strike was totally defeated, and all of the active workers were sacked. This was a period of general industrial discontent, largely because of the wartime trading conditions (see e.g. Maguire 1988). The Ministry of Labour *Weekly Report* for 27 August 1919 notes: 'There has been a marked change during the war in the public attitude towards the profit maker. The socialist cause has in consequence been much strengthened and the view that the individual system of industry is iniquitious and intolerable has spread and intensified among working men.' The seriousness with which the situation was perceived in official circles is confirmed by the following extract from a Treasury sub-committee: 'There is no doubt that there is a considerable feeling throughout the country—a feeling not confined to labour alone, but shared by the bulk of the middle classes—that the supernormal profits of business ... are a proper subject of special taxation.' The role of excess or *supernormal* profits is an important one in Spedan Lewis's rejection of managers' appropriation of huge profits on the basis of equity principles.

In 1928, with the death of his father, Spedan Lewis was able finally to extend the Partnership to the main John Lewis store and institute a proper legal basis for the scheme. The *de jure* ownership of the company was transferred to the workers through the medium of the John Lewis Partnership Trust. The distribution of a share of profits as a bonus was now institutionalized as a right of employees, rather than depending on Spedan Lewis's say-so. This move must have had a substantial impact on the staff's identification with the Partnership.

Previously, the bonus had been paid in the form of a share promise—a concept at two removes from actual cash and undoubtedly quite unfamiliar to the vast majority of the staff. Lewis records in delighted, if somewhat condescending, terms the difficulty partners had in comprehending the full value of their bonus (Lewis 1954: 78). This task must have been somewhat easier after 1929, when the bonus was distributed as negotiable fixed interest non-voting shares. Stock was distributed instead of cash because of the need to preserve the firm's liquidity. In effect, the cash drain was deferred to the future, assuming that a substantial part of the bonus would be liquidated by the partners as soon as possible, as seems plausible. The bonus was a significant amount, as shown in Table 4.2. (Amounts for the years before 1924 are not available.)

TABLE 4.2. *Partnership bonus as percentage of pay, 1924–1929*

Fiscal year	Approximate % of pay
1924	15
1925	20
1926	20
1927	20
1928	23
1929	15

Lewis also experimented with the timing of payment of the bonus. To encourage employees to save a significant part of their bonus, infrequent pay-outs seemed necessary; hence the decision to pay an annual bonus. At a time when shop-workers would find it difficult to save anything substantial out of their pay, the scheme provided a remarkable new opportunity for staff. Once the bonus became a legally instituted right, the tax liability on that portion of profits attached to each individual employee, rather than to Lewis alone. The effect was a significant reduction in the tax paid on the bonus, as many of the partners would not have paid any income tax. The new method was therefore very much more tax-efficient.

The Inauguration of the Partnership: The First Settlement

Almost immediately after the John Lewis Partnership Ltd was established as the sole owner of all shares in John Lewis and Company, the firm was reconstituted as a public company. Three-quarters of a million pounds in additional external capital—needed to fund the acquisition of a neighbouring Oxford Street store, T. J. Harries—was raised in 1928 by issuing fixed dividend stock carrying no voting power. This expansion of property was the first in a large programme of investment, with many purchases apparently made at times when buying prices were low. Evidently the John Lewis Partnership managed to remain financially strong enough to take advantage of opportunities as they arose, at the expense of competitors.

The total number of equity shares of the trading company was 12,000, with each carrying 1,000 votes. The restriction of ownership to the John Lewis Partnership Ltd gave 'control of the Partnership without an important lock up of capital' (Lewis 1954: 65). The irrevocable settlement in trust actually did little more than ensure that the profits went to the partners by stimulating a legal right to those profits.

The terms of transfer of ownership to the staff reflected Lewis's own largesse and implied a major gift to the Partnership. The rough valuation of £1 million was derived from stockbrokers' estimates of the cash worth of John Lewis and Company in the event of a quick sale and therefore almost certainly underestimated the firm's true value. The payment to Lewis took the form of zero interest deferred bonds, to be paid off over 30 years. In effect, John Lewis Partnership was purchased for much less than its true value and in a manner that ensured capital adequacy.

In Lewis's entire account of this change of ownership, there is not the slightest hint that he ever consulted his staff. Beneficiaries of a significant philanthropic gesture, they seem to have been treated like children whose parents were making provision for their adulthood. Lewis's view of the whole enterprise as an experiment inevitably reduced the *partners* somewhat to the level of laboratory rats, albeit rather well-endowed ones. Nominal ownership did not at this stage confer any effective power.

From 1929 to the Present

In the decades that followed the initial settlement in trust, the John Lewis Partnership grew, absorbed other firms, and became a major retailer in the United Kingdom. Tested in a business context, the Partnership Principles were found to work. Although the business development of the Partnership was severely set back by the damage sustained during the Second World War, the post-war period saw long-term recovery.

Expansion and Development

The John Lewis Partnership grew rapidly, reflecting both prudence and good fortune. It is clear that pay-outs of Partnership benefits were never allowed to absorb funds needed for investment in expansion. Spedan Lewis retained total control of the business affairs of the Partnership and could ignore the partners' wish for higher benefit payments if he chose. During 1933 and 1934, stores were purchased in Nottingham, Weston-super-Mare, Southsea, and

Southampton. Most of these stores were regarded as derelicts: poor businesses to be improved by the application of Partnership Principles.

A more significant acquisition was the purchase of the Oxford Street site of D. H. Evans, adjacent to John Lewis's store. This acquisition provided not only an excellent opportunity to consolidate the flagship store, but also some extra insurance in wartime. As early as 1934 the Partnership had adopted a policy of attempting to disperse its property as a precaution against air raids during war. In the event, the main John Lewis shop was severely damaged in an air raid; continued trading was possible only because of the acquisition of the D. H. Evans site and the 1928 purchase of the T. J. Harries store.

In 1940 a major step was taken with the purchase for only £30,000 of a controlling interest in Selfridge Provincial Stores Ltd. Some £3 million of capital had been invested in this company over the years, but it was in poor commercial condition. The Partnership acquired fifteen new stores and a new, more geographically dispersed retail network. Six of the stores were in London and the remainder outside, thus providing a further hedge against war damage. Turnover of the whole Partnership rose by around 60 per cent as a result of this deal. Once again the acquisition of new stores in bad condition afforded an opportunity for the Partnership Principles solution. Each store was admitted to Partnership benefit as it improved its position. But it appears that motivations went beyond purely financial incentives. Lewis, evidently adhering to certain constructive aspects of his father's business practices, records the crucial role of service: 'It would be difficult to exaggerate the extent to which the general helpfulness, that developed quite fast between the new partners and their new Management, was due simply to the pleasure of the new partners in finding themselves giving much better service to their customers' (Lewis 1954: 120). The conflict between paying out Partnership profits immediately and reinvesting for future rewards came to the surface at this time, but was apparently not squarely faced.

The traditional literature predicts that employee-owned companies will tend to underinvest and overdistribute profits in the short term: since only a fraction of the current membership will enjoy future benefits, they will tend to prefer current pay-outs. Lewis explicitly raises the possibility that some partners might vote against expansion schemes, but falls back on the idea of managers taking the longer, more prudent view. Awareness of this potential problem presumably informed Lewis's attitude to partners' participation. This was summarized in the principle that they should be kept at arms' length from strategic decisions and should be encouraged as much as possible to think carefully about these matters in the hope of their supporting the *right* course of action.

Since the John Lewis Partnership is purportedly owned and run by and for both current and future partners, it is important to come to terms with this characteristic problem of collective ownership. In the John Lewis Partnership case it was resolved by the deliberate institutional prevention of any truly effective partnership of power. Lewis clearly believed this was a necessary condition for the long-term success of an employee-owned firm.

In the first decade or so after the 1929 settlement, the Partnership expanded its welfare benefits, driven by the imaginative enthusiasm of Spedan Lewis. Little if any pressure for these schemes seems to have come from the shop-floor; Lewis himself identified areas of need and then acted on them. (This is not to say that the benefits were necessarily any less welcome.) Somewhat in the spirit of an amateur (in a strict, non-pejorative sense) scientist conducting social engineering experiments, Lewis entertained expansive hopes for partnership-related activities. His keeness to set up education establishments suggest a comparison with Robert Owen and his New Lanark experiments which presumed that productive efficiency was engendered by investments in social welfare programmes. However, Lewis's vision was rather less utopian and all encompassing.

During the 1930s collective pressure for greater security in working people's lives grew and eventually dominated national politics. Oddly, the economic depression of the period is barely mentioned in Lewis's account of the development of the John Lewis Partnership, suggesting that the firm was not very severely affected. (Some protection was presumably provided by its concentration in the south-east of the country and its particular appeal to the burgeoning middle class.) Quite possibly the partners were relatively unaffected also. The John Lewis Partnership may have helped them to ride out this period in relative security and affluence.

The Post-war Period

The Partnership emerged from the Second World War in rather poor financial shape. Its profitability was lower than for the sector as a whole and for publicly quoted department stores. The major drain on resources was the need to rebuild fixed assets, largely property. The war had done major damage to the flagship store in Oxford Street in London. Trading continued in a reduced manner, through the other stores that had been acquired during the 1930s.

In 1947 Conservative Member of Parliament Ernest Marples published *The Road to Prosperity; An Industrial Policy*, as part of an attempt to rescue what he called progressive conservatism. The book enthusiastically endorses a form of industrial co-partnership in which an agreed proportion of profits is shared with employees, who are enabled and encouraged to acquire capital in the firm and are granted a share in management. Marples cites several British examples of each of these features in action, individually and in combination. It is striking that he never mentions the John Lewis Partnership. All in all, the John Lewis Partnership seems to have been in some difficulty at the time. The Partnership entered the long post-war boom period from a poor starting point.

Completion of the Partnership: The Second Settlement

In 1950, when trading had recovered from war conditions and the payment of Partnership bonus had resumed, the second trust settlement was made, completing Lewis's organizational vision. The full voting power of the shares in the Partnership was transferred to the trustees of the John Lewis Partnership Trust Ltd and a constitutional basis was established for the operation of Partnership Principles. To follow Lewis's own analogy, the second trust settlement marked the achievement of a constitutional monarchy, with all partners fully enfranchised through an institutional structure that had the trustees at its apex.

Pushing the analogy further, the two settlements of 1929 and 1950 can be likened to two great reform bills in the evolution of a new model of business democracy. Yet neither move was made in response to actual or potential pressure or agitation from the workers. On the contrary, both settlements reflected the vision and benignly comprehensive power of the founder, Spedan Lewis. It is difficult to say just how far Lewis himself would have seen this pattern as characteristic of human progress, but it seems plausible that he placed more faith in paternalistic reform than in a dialectical resolution of conflicts arising out of the growing strength of organized labour.

The reliance on a constitutional model of business organization is significant in itself, quite apart from the democratic content of the constitution. This approach reflects a belief that conflict in the firm can generally be avoided and that there is another common ground for the management and workers to agree to the legitimacy of certain ground rules. A constitution goes beyond a simple declaration of principles or intentions, which may be found in many firms—generally observed by managers but overridden as commercial exigencies seem to require. Lewis's model is an attempt to set up the rules of the game together with adjudicators. As a practical matter, the chairman seems to have been assigned the role of judge, but the trustees and an internal system of registrars also play important roles. As an ultimate institutional safeguard against abuse of power by the chairman, the trustees have the power to remove him or her.

The constitutional structure of the John Lewis Partnership is discussed in greater detail below. It reflects Lewis's sense that a civilized and fair form of capitalism could be achieved. Besides articulating principles for running the firm itself, the constitution enjoins the Partnership to observe certain decent and fair standards of behaviour towards its competitors and suppliers. Lewis evidently

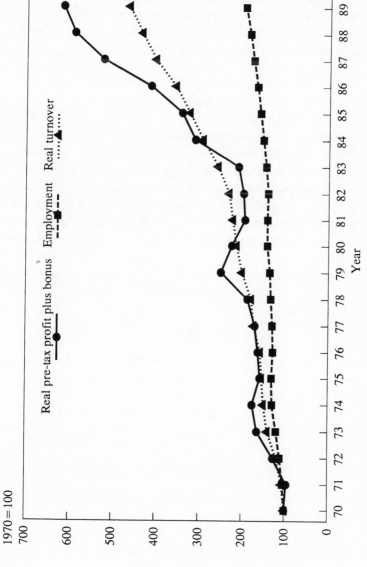

1970 = 100

Real pre-tax profit plus bonus ●

Employment ■

Real turnover ▲

FIG. 4.1. Real pre-tax profits, real sales, and employment, 1970–1989

hoped that other firm owners would learn from the example of the Partnership.

As Figure 4.1 shows, the John Lewis Partnership's sales rose rapidly in real terms. Real profits and employment levels also rose between 1970 and 1989, the period of the main comparative study undertaken below.

Conclusion

Over the last thirty years the John Lewis Partnership has compiled a record of steady long-term growth and stability, of which a conventional firm could be quite proud. The employee-ownership system appears to work, at least when judged by the criterion of commercial survival. The operation of the Partnership, in particular its business performance, is the theme of the next three chapters, which begin with a detailed examination of its organizational structure.

5

The Organizational Structure in 1989

Introduction

The formal institutions of power, information, and accountability at the John Lewis Partnership have not changed significantly since the early 1950s. In this chapter they will be described and contrasted with those of a stereotypical capital-owned firm. We will also consider the form of industrial democracy on which the Partnership rests.

The Institutions of Partnership

Since 1950, the full ownership rights of the John Lewis Partnership have been vested in the John Lewis Partnership Trust Ltd, which owns all shares in the various sections of the Partnership. This company is controlled in normal circumstances by its chairman, who holds all the votes except in particular circumstances. The board comprises a deputy chairman and three trustees appointed by the Central Council, a predominantly elected body which links the individual partners and the very top of the decision-making tree.

The Trust is not the normal locus of management power, however. The constitution sets out three components of what it calls *principal management*. The first and most important of these is the chairman of the Trust, who is also chairman of the Partnership itself. He or she presides over the Central Board, the second element, whose members are nominated by either the chairman or the Central Council, the third element in the management structure. The Central Board is therefore the main decision-making committee, but the chairman is the main centre of power at an operational level. Of the eleven other members of the Central Board, six (including the deputy chairman) are chosen by the chairman and five by the Council. There is thus a strong suggestion of Cabinet government, with the Board containing a built-in majority of people likely to be predisposed towards the chairman's point of view. A subset of this Board is the Principal Executive Committee, which discusses policy and advises the chairman. In effect, the chairman is largely free to arrange the affairs of the Partnership at the executive level.

Since the chairman is appointed by his predecessor, there is likely to be a great deal of continuity in the management of the John Lewis Partnership, which may in itself be important in explaining the survival of the Lewis ideals and the Partnership itself. It is clear that the chairman is, as Lewis's successor put it, '... in normal circumstances, in full control of the operations of the Partnership'. In this respect, his position resembles that of a joint chairman and chief executive in a more conventional firm, with perhaps even greater power, since the board is unlikely to outvote him and there are no shareholders to face, other than the Central Board itself and its representatives on the Central Board. With no external voting shareholders, moreover, the discipline of potential take-overs is absent. Because the John Lewis Partnership is largely self-financed, there is very little risk associated with financial leverage from outside.

The chairman's actions are to some extent constrained by the Partnership's mechanism for ensuring adequate management accountability. Spedan Lewis's conception of democratic rights hinges on the right to be represented. Representation could mean solely the right to voice discontent, without any direct participation in power, or it could involve the right to vote for or otherwise influence the executive. Lewis seems to lean towards the former view, at least as far as industrial democracy goes. This approach presupposes that the management will in general take notice of what the employees' representatives have to say, particularly if there is a constitutional imperative that they do so. Any need for partners to be represented in the second sense gets little attention in Lewis's writings.

The John Lewis Partnership system of representation has at its apex the Central Council, intended to be the forum and focus of public opinion in the Partnership. Up to one-fifth of its 140 members are appointed by the chairman, giving still more power to the executive but also ensuring some continuity in the Council. These appointees are typically selected from the ranks of senior management (Flanders *et al.* 1968). The remaining Council members are elected by the entire Partnership in an exercise of an apparently genuine democratic nature.

The Central Council has two related functions. First, it raises issues for formal but open discussion with senior management; these matters may have been suggested directly by partners at shop-floor level. Second, the Council is assigned certain (largely negative) powers beyond its role in electing trustees and members of the Central Board; for example, it can veto amendments to the constitution. A large representative body such as this could not readily play a direct part in executive decision-making, but the leverage of the Council over the Board is apparently rather less than say that of Parliament over the Cabinet. The Council appointees to the Board have the right to demand that certain issues be brought to the Council's notice for discussion, including major redundancies or changes in the capital structure; on the whole, however, the power of the Council lies in simply confronting management on important issues.

The Council is backed up by a number of other representative institutions. Branch Councils link partners rather more closely to the Central Council. Committees for Communication organize discussions between rank-and-file members and their management. These are relatively informal meetings, though minutes are taken and replies can be requested from senior managers. A principal director of the John Lewis Partnership is designated as the partner's counsellor and presides over the Committees for Communication. A system of registrars is intended to police observarion of the constitution.

The structure of representation is reinforced by a well-developed system of information flows, derived from the John Lewis Partnership principle that sharing of knowledge is a crucial part of the Partnership. An extensive series of internal publications makes it easy to raise all types of issues and requires an acceptable response from management. Anonymity is permitted, to encourage frankness. The Partnership's internal journalism operates as a form of continuing employee opinion audit, keeping management abreast of concerns among the partners.

Together, the Partnership's representative structures, which can confront management with grievances or simply ask questions, buttressed by two-way flows of information in the internal press, appear to constitute a credible system of accountability. This is one of the most distinctive features of the John Lewis Partnership, although it is not quite what most observers would describe as industrial democracy. However, the two are not incompatible. Within limits, the John Lewis Partnership approach to management accountability may also be compatible with a more conventional ownership structure.

Industrial Democracy at the John Lewis Partnership

If the John Lewis Partnership is described as an experiment in industrial democracy, what is one to make of the role of the chairman? The extensive powers of the executive have been described above; the question is whether the role of the trustees is such as to provide *genuine* democracy at the John Lewis Partnership.

Although in many respects the John Lewis Partnership chairmanship is an almost dynastic autocracy, it is subject to one final sanction. If the Central Council judges that the chairman has failed to uphold the constitution in some respect, or that he has failed to pay dividends, then it can instigate a procedure that in theory would allow the Council to replace the chairman. (To do so, however, the trustees would have to gain 60 per cent of the votes in the Trust.) This provision would constitute a serious check on the chairman's power, except that it is so unlikely ever to be invoked. In fact, the mechanism could almost have been designed to give the impression that the partners, via the Central Council, have control, but at the least possible operational inconvenience to the chairman. In effect, the Partnership's underlying philosophy is that the establishment of a constitutional framework for power, together with ample opportunities for confronting the management on issues of concern to workers, is both necessary and sufficient to achieve an acceptable level of democracy in the firm, subject to the constraint that commercial aims be met.

This view is reinforced by former Chairman Sir Bernard Miller's assertion that: 'Any viable system of industrial democracy must take account of the fact that most people no more want to govern themselves than to be their own doctors or lawyers (Flanders *et al.* 1968: 18). Miller shares Spedan Lewis's conviction that effective democracy is fundamentally a matter of the manager's account-ability to the managed. The ethos is well expressed by Miller:

The partners do not choose their management ... but unless the management secures and retains the backing of the general opinion of the Partnership, it will be unable to manage the Partnership efficiently and risk being in breach of the constitution and so liable to displacement. In that specific case, the partners, through their elected representatives, do choose their management. (Flanders *et al.* 1969: 17)

It could be argued that any firm suffers if the management does not enjoy the backing of the workforce. Because the Partnership Principles are enshrined in a formal constitution at the John Lewis Partnership, however, it would be a particularly serious develop-ment for the chairman to lose the backing of the partners. A chairman chosen by his predecessor presumably will be committed to the Partnership Principles, and will adhere to the letter and spirit of the constitution, so that the partners will never have occasion to exercise their right of negative sanction. In this sense, the ability of the trustees to remove the chairman is largely superfluous except in so far as it makes transparent the ultimate ownership of the company. This aspect of governance boils down to a sort of legitimation function that may be critical to the smooth operation of the John Lewis Partnership but is not in itself an operationally relevant instrument of industrial democracy in the normal sense of that expression.

What Is Distinctive About the John Lewis Partnership?

Table 5.1 compares the John Lewis Partnership with a stereotypical conventional firm along several dimensions. The John Lewis Partnership's own competitors are not necessarily like this hypothetical conventional firm—Marks and Spencer, for example, is markedly more paternalistic than the average employer. In some respects as Table 5.1 suggests, the John Lewis Partnership is truly distinct from other firms; in others the differences are more a matter of degree.

The three most unusual features of the John Lewis Partnership are:

1. It has a constitutional structure that governs management–worker relations. Although this constitution was established by a former owner of the firm, it gains legitimacy from being adjudicated by a representative council, mostly elected by the workforce.
2. The management of the Partnership does not face any risk of take over and are therefore protected from the most important form of discipline recognized in the modern theory of the firm. However, the employees have the right in principle to remove the chairman (and chief executive) in extreme circumstances. This right may function more on the level of legitimation than of practical power, but it is clearly a different sort of sanction from the contingent ability of a unionized workforce to inflict severe strike damage, for example.
3. Employees' remuneration includes a significant share that is related directly to trading success. Although not regarded officially as pay, but as something separate and additional, this benefit is a material difference from most other firms, even if the gap is perhaps closing slowly.

TABLE 5.1. *Characteristics of the John Lewis Partnership and a stereotypical conventional firm*

Company characteristic	Stereotypical conventional firm	John Lewis Partnership
Objectives		
Ultimate ownership	Shareholders	Partners (past, present, future)
Company objectives	Profit	Present value of the Trust = profit
Constraints		
Management accountability	External shareholders	All employees
Capital market discipline	Potentially high: considerable take-over risk	Very low: zero take-over risk
Product market discipline	High: increasingly competitive market	High: increasingly competitive market
Labour issues		
Profit-share in relation to pay	Minimal, if at all	Substantial
Role of training	Varied: generally limited	Central and strategic
Grievance procedures	Workplace group or union-based	Committees plus representation
Structure of control	Managerially determined	Constitutional
Organization and culture		
Legitimation of management	Power and competence	Constitutional
Corporate culture	Varied, often weak	Particular and strong

Conclusion

Today the John Lewis Partnership is less unusual than it once was: many firms now use some sort of profit-sharing mechanism, although they normally distribute much smaller amounts of money in this way. The Partnership's practices with respect to employee participation and in-firm communication are also less unusual than they used to be; it remains to see how far this development is a transient fashion and how far a major change in the organization of work.

In certain respects, therefore, the Partnership is distinctive only in degree. But in other respects it is quite different in kind from other firms. First, the fact that managers are immune to take over are largely independent of capital market discipline is of major importance; as we will show, the firm lacks an attribute conventionally considered very important for successful performance. Second, workers as partners have a significant influence on the decision-takers in the Partnership, if only because of their right to remove the chairman. This is a striking contrast with the vast majority of other firms, and especially the Partnership's own competitors. In the conventional view, this characteristic would be expected to have an almost entirely negative effect on company performance, as discussed below.

6

Existing Research on the John Lewis Partnership

Introduction

The John Lewis Partnership has been an object of interest for many years. This chapter examines some of the main findings of studies undertaken in the last two decades, covering the issues of industrial democracy, participation, and labour market indicators. The main work is that of Flanders, Pomeranz, and Woodward, a major study conducted in the late 1960s. Subsequent work has tended to follow Flanders *et al.* in concentrating on the issue of participation and industrial democracy. Only in very recent years has there been a move to considering the Partnership centrally as a commercial business organization. Research has also been carried out on the Weitzman-type effects of the bonus payment.

Experiment in Industrial Democracy: Flanders, Pomeranz, and Woodward

Method and theory

In 1968 Flanders *et al.* published a book entitled *Experiment in Industrial Democracy: A Study of the John Lewis Partnership*. The first part of the title is taken from Spedan Lewis's own description of what the Partnership was all about. The authors intended to investigate how this experiment affected the people working in it.

That the John Lewis Partnership has succeeded commercially is not in doubt, but what can be learnt from its experience about the possibility and the value of introducing democratic principles and institutions into business organisation? To this critical question, which has long been debated without being satisfactorily resolved, the study is addressed. (Flanders *et al.* 1968: 23)

Flanders *et al.* asked such questions as whether the workers were interested in the opportunities to share in the profits and management of the firm, how they valued these opportunities, and whether these opportunities affected attitudes to work and to the employer. In short, the authors were interested in 'what the Partnership means to the Partners' (Flanders *et al.* 1958: 23). To the extent that the lessons learned from studying the John Lewis Partnership can be generalized to other firms, the effects of the Partnership institutions on business performance and on the general welfare of all concerned are of considerable interest.

Flanders *et al.* do not directly conceptualize the *value* of institutional innovation, however. They beg the question *of value to whom?*—or rather answer it only implicitly. The three main groups who might benefit are shareholders, employees' and managers. In the John Lewis Partnership, the first group overlaps with the second and third, and we are left with the distinction between managers and workers. Flanders *et al.* rely heavily on this dichotomy, without providing any theoretical discussion as to how precisely the two categories differ.

Such questions as Flanders *et al.* investigate can be addressed coherently only in the context of some comparison, either with a priori expectations derived from theory, or with other relevant institutions. The authors implicitly chose the former route, since their survey uses no control. (The practical obstacles to doing so would have been considerable.) Instead the authors' thinking is guided by a theoretical framework regarding the nature of industrial democracy. The underlying theme of the book is that some minimum set of conditions must be met for the genuine practice of industrial democracy, and that these conditions are not all found in the John Lewis Partnership. Consequently, the experiment is judged, although not in so many words, to have been a failure, or more accurately to have been mislabelled. It is clear that the management of the Partnership would not accept this assumption. In the book's carefully worded foreword, the then Chairman, Sir Bernard Miller, comments: 'The authors have quite naturally formulated their own definitions of the aims and functions of industrial democracy and have judged the Partnership's value as an experiment in industrial democracy against these. It should however be judged also against the aims and intention with which it was created' (Flanders *et al.* 1968: 21).

Flanders *et al.* adopt roughly the following view of the business organization: the ends of a business are necessarily economic, but the means, involving as they do a hierarchy of power and a rule of law backed by the sanction of sacking, are at least in part necessarily political. Thus a series of political questions arise: How far is the power of the managers or owners arbitrary? What are the restraints on this power? What are the rights and freedoms of employees? What are the grievance procedures? Since every business needs some political system to control its employees, there is always a system of managerial control, which includes means of persuasion the influencing of motivation, the direction of work, and some form of communication system.

With this in mind, the authors then consider the meaning of industrial democracy, which they recognize 'is a highly controversial subject' (Flanders *et al.* 1968: 27). As a bare minimum, they argue, democracy must meet the following conditions:

1. Management may not act arbitrarily.
2. Employees must have some control over matters that concern them directly.

These conditions are both met in the case of the John Lewis Partnership. However, Flanders *et al.* argue that industrial democracy must also involve what they call a system of democratic control, operating from the bottom up (in contrast to the top-down management control system). The two control systems intersect and interact, often sharing the same institutions and possibly in harmony for much of the time. This third condition is found to be wanting in the John Lewis Partnership—primarily, the authors believe, because the system has from the start been designed and implemented by management.

Industrial democracy that originates at the top, rather than arising from grass roots, is judged to be suspicious and possibly bogus: 'The two principal sources of industrial democracy—where something of it can be said to exist in present-day industry—are the work group and the trade union; the one resting on informal and the other on formal organization; the one internal to the organization of the firm, the other external' (Flanders *et al.* 1968: 29). Thus the authors bring to their study an a priori scepticism as to whether the Partnership truly constitutes an industrial democracy worthy of the name. They see problems in the imposition of the system from above:

There are the possible dangers of paternalism. Assumptions may be made about the ways in which employees would like to participate in management, and so protect their interests, which do not correspond with their actual preferences. This is the crux of the dilemma posed by the choice between the growth of industrial democracy from above and from below. (Flanders *et al.* 1968: 30)

This approach may make too much of an issue of the meaning of industrial democracy. The fact that Spedan Lewis used the term himself is not necessarily very relevant. More to the point, perhaps, are his explicitly expressed views about the role of employees in business and the way in which ethical principles and business practice can be reconciled. These statements form a sort of theory of which the John Lewis Partnership is an institutional embodiment, and against which its success could have been measured. In any case, the term *industrial democracy* has changed its meaning considerably since it was used by Spedan Lewis. (Such semantic evolution is by no means unusual: consider what *social democratic* meant earlier this century.) When the John Lewis Partnership was first set up, there was no welfare state and very little legal protection for labour other than the basic trade union immunities—of limited value in retailing, which has historically been very weakly unionized. Lewis's ideas were radical for their time and justified the use of radical lanaguage.

In a sense, then, the considerations of Flanders *et al.* were a virtually inevitable consequence of the analytic framework they adopted. A further weakness is their failure to place their findings in a business context. Nevertheless, their empirical findings are of considerable interest.

Findings

As a general point, Flanders *et al.* note that roles at the John Lewis Partnership are made much more explicit (defined in the constitution) than are relationships. There is little concept of an organizational structure. This ambiguity offers certain advantages of flexibility, but at the cost of frequent discrepancies between formal and informal patterns of interaction. This flexibility helps explain how a firm could survive commercially for 75 years with apparently the same organizational structure set out in print.

The Committees for Communication, one of the oldest of the Partnership institutions, are essentially grievance settling bodies, rather than a two-way channel for direct exchange of information between the top and the bottom of the hierarchy. They cannot take remedial action themselves, but bring matters to the attention of managers, who then take action. In the partners' perception, they *tend to get things done* and appear to be successful as grievance mechanisms.

Examining the composition of the elected bodies, Flanders *et al.* find that rank-and-file workers are not well represented on the Central Council. Over the period 1958–67 rank-and-file workers made up an average of 11 per cent of the Council, while managers' share was 68 per cent. (The remainder of the Council consists of ex officio managerial members, chosen by the chairman.) The authors conclude that the Central Council 'in terms of status is a predominantly management body' (Flanders *et al.* 1968: 60). The pattern is still more extreme on the committees that carry out much of the Council's work. (Spedan Lewis modelled his organization loosely on the Parliamentary Select Committee system.)

The composition of these committees is 'markedly in favour of the higher rather than the lower managerial grades'. Ex officio members play a larger role on these committees also (Flanders *et al.* 1968: 61). In the Branch Councils, on the other hand, rank-and-file partners represent about half the membership, and only about 15 per cent are ex officio members.

The authors conclude that the committee and council system rests heavily 'on accountability of management to the managed as a central feature of its democracy, and its excellent committee network is designed to foster the free exchange of information and views between those responsible for decisions and all the other workers in the organisation' (Flanders *et al.* 1968: 76). The underlying theory is correctly described; this was indeed Spedan Lewis's conception of democracy in a commercial organization. Given that conception, the system is judged to work effectively.

Flanders *et al.* find that the system has a quite positive effect on management:

1. The system inculcates a strong sense of responsibility among managers at all levels, encouraging a high commitment to organisational goals and the welfare of members (p. 183).
2. It reinforces the authority of management: strong moral justification adds to their power, which is not constrained by the need to act for shareholders in the conventional way; this leads to greater security for management and a strong sense of legitimacy, based on knowledge, equal handedness and hard work (p. 184).
3. The *ideology* of the Partnership compensates for loose organisation and facilitates flexibility.

The overall conclusion on management is a strongly affirmative one: 'Granted that the commercial success of any large business enterprise depends first and foremost on its management, the reasons for the commercial success of the John Lewis Partnership are not hard to find' (Flanders *et al.* 1968: 185).

The effects on non-managerial employees are seen as less favourable. The Councils exercise powers in ways not very different from the practice of other firms. The high proportion of managerial membership, moreover, diminishes the Councils' impact. The Committees for Communication and the activities of the registrars and partners' counsellor: 'undoubtedly provide an effective means of prompting management not to neglect the human side of its problems and enabling the rank and file to raise their complaints. Even so it is not, and was never intended to be, a democratic control over management' (Flanders *et al.* 1968: 187). Although this conclusion is correct, it assumes an unduly large role in the authors' judgement of the *value* of the John Lewis Partnership. The control of management by accountability is acknowledged to be 'a real and all-pervading power'. But Flanders *et al.* regard the John Lewis Partnership as a case of government of the people, rather than government by the people—and thus not an instance of industrial democracy (Flanders *et al.* 1968: 187).

Flanders *et al.* find considerable variation in the effect of Partnership institutions on employee attitudes. They divide their sample into two groups, one showing a high degree of interest in the institutions of the Partnership, the other a low degree of interest. This criterion is used as a proxy for involvement. Among partners with at least five years' service these two categories are roughly equal in size.

The two groups show appreciable differences in job satisfaction and in general attitudes to the employer. However, they show no consistent differences in attitudes to personnel policies such as relations to supervisors, profit-sharing, or security of employment. The overall conclusion of the attitude survey is that the orientation of most employees remains essentially *calculative* rather than *normative* (see e.g. Etzioni 1961). Employees regard the firm as a *good employer*. Except for a small minority, their attitude does not 'entail any commitment to the Partnership's ideology' (Flanders *et al.*: 190). In general, their job satisfaction is roughly comparable to that recorded in the national sample of the working population: 'While the Partnership is rated highly as an employer, concerned with the partners' security and welfare, it comes in for a fair amount of criticism from the rank and file, essentially on the grounds that they have not enough say in settling pay and working conditions' (Flanders *et al.* 1968: 190). Satisfaction indices are always relative to some prior expectation of what would be normal or acceptable.

There is an inevitable risk that the Partnership's rhetoric and the appearance of considerable participation will heighten involvement and employee expectations, only to frustrate those partners who wish actually to take part in managerial decision-making.

Flanders *et al.* adhere to a particular conception of how industrial democracy is likely to arise and flourish, emphasizing the growth of pressure from the shop-floor. They note that the Partnership ideology is a barrier to pressure groups building up from below. The system therefore prevents significant evolutionary pressure from being effective. But cumulative suppression would be expected to lead to some catastrophic outcome, either a strike or a collapse of morale. Flanders *et al.* find no evidence of such a build-up, suggesting that they have perhaps exaggerated the inflexibility of the system.

Flanders *et al.* followed the process by which the Partnership chose to begin opening five days a week, a matter of direct interest to partners. Their comments on management style are of some interest: 'No one reading our account could possibly doubt top management's sincerity in trying to find a solution which would meet with general consent' (Flanders *et al.* 1968: 191). And yet, at the end, a decision was reached by a process which was 'basically the normal one of management deciding what it wanted to achieve, and preparing the ground in such a way that orders issued were likely to be obeyed' (Flanders *et al.* 1968: 176).

Judged by the authors' standards of industrial democracy, this episode may sound like a failure, but as a lesson in effective management it is of considerable significance. If John Lewis Partnership managers can reconcile concern for employees with the achievement of their strategic objectives, this ought to give the firm a significant commercial advantage. In addition, it appears that the Partnership has created the conditions for a generally happy workforce. The arrangements for sharing of gain and of knowledge and the associated institutions of Partnership 'have made the employment relationship positively attractive for most employees' (Flanders *et al.* 1968: 192).

Employee Participation in the John Lewis Partnership

Dodd (1972) investigates employee participation in the John Lewis Partnership, using the following two-part definition of participation:

1. employees are encouraged to use the opportunities within the concern for increased fulfilment of their interests and abilities and
2. to take part (through representatives or directly) in its management at all levels (Dodd 1972: 5).

Dodd's work, like that of Flanders *et al.*, is a product of its time and is concerned to establish that the John Lewis Partnership does not match up to his criterion of participation. The first, more general part of the definition reflects the notion that a logical and proper counterpart of wider citizenship rights should be an enriched life at work. Such enrichment is sought both for its own sake and as a possible spur to greater productivity. In the latter case. Dodd places considerable faith in the idea of job enrichment, drawing on the ideas of Herzberg (1968).

The second part of the definition is closer to the ideal of the worker co-operative, emphasizing a shared management of the firm's activities. It is also directly ruled out by the whole philosophy of the John Lewis Partnership as reflected in Spedan Lewis's business principles (see below). By this definition, accordingly, it is a foregone conclusion that the John Lewis Partnership will be judged not to be a participatory firm. This is precisely Dodd's conclusion. He argues that the mechanism of removing the chairman is very unlikely ever to be used because: (i) the firm is 'a relatively prosperous concern' and (ii) the constitution was created by past and present management and so the chairman is unlikely to fail to uphold it. This raises two points. First, the source of the relative prosperity is not enquired into, nor is it discussed relative to some of the author's proposed radical changes (see below). Second, the constitution was created by Spedan Lewis and survives substantially intact. Subsequent chairmen are highly restricted in their freedom of manoeuvre outside the constitution, whether they like it or not. This was precisely as intended: the sanction of sacking the chairman is supposed to uphold this state of affairs.

Dodd argues further that the accountability of management is less impressive than it appears since managers could always reduce their accountability if they chose. In fact, the constitutional safeguards would virtually rule out such a change, but Dodd's argument misses the point once again that the Partnership is founded on the right to be represented and the duty of management to be accountable. Dodd notes that most of the company's internal publications are concerned with welfare measures rather than management matters. He interprets this orientation as further evidence that the John Lewis Partnership cannot be considered a participatory firm.

In conclusion then, Dodd judges that his second criterion— that employees participate in management—is definitely not met. Going further, he argues that the first criterion is not satisfied either, primarily because the Partnership does not offer job-enrichment schemes that might increase the interest of the work. Consequently, the John Lewis Partnership emerges as a fairly typical employer. By way of remedy, Dodd proposes that executive decision-making be delegated to the central council, beginning with personnel matters, including pay and the size of the bonus, and proceeding to all management affairs. The Council's decisions would be 'subject to the final control of the chairman' (Dodd 1972: 23). It is not clear how a large body such as the Council could take on this task. Presumably it would have to set up sub-committees to handle the problem, with the chairman present. The result would resemble the existing system, unless the Council had some line veto power over final decisions. Such changes would almost certainly undermine one of the greatest strengths of the Partnership, its ability to keep management unencumbered by committees.

Dodd's enthusiasm for *genuine* participation and job enrichment is partly a reflection of concerns that were prominent at the time of his research. His failure to consider the business side of the John Lewis Partnership, let alone to investigate whether the proposed changes would keep the firm viable in financial terms, reflects a widespread shortcoming of organizational studies that focus on commercial concerns. The overriding consideration for any firm is whether it can survive financially; everything else has to be considered in that context.

Corporate Paternalism

More recently Udo (1986) has investigated the John Lewis Partnership as an employer, comparing it with Marks and Spencer, which has long had a reputation for a paternalistic attitude to its staff. A goal of the study was to identify *Japanese* working practices in United Kingdom firms. These practices are taken to be synonymous with paternalism, which is never explicitly defined, but appears to mean in this context:

1. management–worker communication systems;
2. a high degree of worker participation; and
3. concern for staff welfare.

Interestingly, Udo compares the experience of part-time workers in the two firms. The use of part-time workers in retailing is driven primarily by the employer's need for flexibility. As a result, such workers tend to have poorer security and benefits. This is largely a matter of bargaining power: the typical part-time worker has been female and young, often just entering the workforce. The two firms differ considerably in their use of part-time workers. In 1984 Marks and Spencer employed 18,754 full-timers, with 32,152 part-timers; the John Lewis Partnership had 20,760 full-timers and 6,309 part-timers in 1985. It is important to note that the Partnership bonus and benefits are paid to part-time workers, so long as they are permanent employees, so there is no formal discrimination. However, workers under 19 are deemed to be temporary (Udo 1986: 16).

Udo points to two reasons for the John Lewis Partnership's much lower proportion of part-timers:

1. They are more costly in terms of certain items such as the free uniforms provided and a number of other welfare benefits.

2. There are problems in training them to the same degree of product knowledge as full-timers.

Presumably it is also more difficult to instil a strong sense of partnership principles in part-time workers.

Udo found that both firms paid a rate that was well ahead of the average, as given in the New Earnings Survey. When the bonus was added as well, the John Lewis Partnership partners: 'take their pay well above the earnings of their contemporaries in other retail trade organisations' (Udo 1986: 19). Udo concludes that the material benefits of working as a part-timer at John Lewis Partnership are considerable and are better than those at Marks and Spencer. The John Lewis Partnership also offered more extensive training, covering not just till training and computerized stock control but also 'the servicing of customers' as an activity to be learned in its own right.

Pay and Career Development

Udo's findings are similar to those reported in Bradley, Estrin, and Taylor (1990), which investigates in more detail the comparative benefits and career development prospects for both shop assistants and management trainees in a range of high street stores, including the John Lewis Partnership. In that study, the John Lewis Partnership emerges as one of the most attractive employers among the large *first-division* retailers. Pay, excluding the bonus, was found to be at the top of the range, and the training and career structure appear to be well worked out. Only Marks and Spencer, who have a reputation for effective personnel policies, were found to operate at a comparable level.

In interviewing prospective employees, recruiters at the Partnership emphasized the firm's distinctive ownership and participation structure. In particular, potential management trainees were made fully aware of the nature of the participatory environment. Bradley *et al.* conclude that 'this seems to confirm the view that the John Lewis Partnership management is self-selected to

conform with the relatively more democratic organizational structure' (p. 20).

Two other facts about the Partnership's employment policy and
personnel strategy stand out from this study. First, the turnover of
John Lewis Partnership staff is unusually low; the rate stood at 7.1
per cent in the first six months of 1984–5, whereas figures of up
to 30 per cent are quite common in retailing. Second, the use of
part-time workers is considerably lower in the Partnership than in
the comparator companies of Sainsbury and Marks and Spencer.
Figure 6.1 shows the relative position: Marks and Spencer used
around double the proportion of part-time workers by the end of
the period.

Weitzman Effects

The influential work of Weitzman (1984; 1986; 1987) on the
potential of profit-sharing for promoting employment stability and
reducing inflation has stimulated cross-sectional investigations of
his hypothesis (Blanchflower and Oswald 1987). Bradley and Estrin
(1987) use evidence from the John Lewis Partnership on the impact
of profit-sharing. Their main conclusions are the following:

1. Profit-sharing in the John Lewis Partnership acts to raise wage
flexibility, in that a bonus payment will vary more than a base
wage for firm-specific and broader market conditions.
2. This has not brought advantages in terms of reduced fluctuations
in employment over the trade cycle; Bradley and Estrin suggest
that this problem may be endemic to the retail sector with its high
flexibility of staff and relatively high turnover.
3. Profit-sharing in the John Lewis Partnership can be associated
with significantly higher levels of employment for given product
market conditions and rates of pay; this difference, according to
the authors, is likely to be due to a Weitzman-type enhanced labour
demand effect, rather than solely to motivational factors.

This study does not directly extend this line of enquiry.

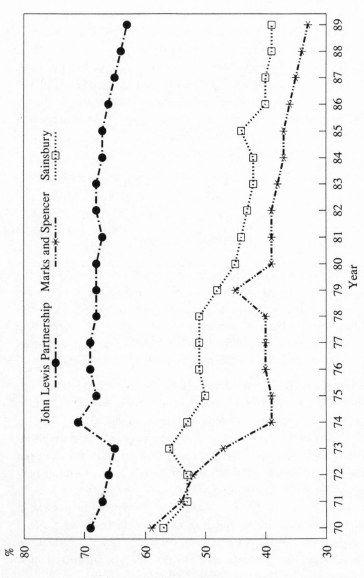

FIG. 6.1.　Full-time workers as a percentage of total, 1970–1989

Conclusion

Most research on the John Lewis Partnership has not directly enquired how the institution survives as a commercial concern in a market economy. However, the findings of the various studies suggest that the emphasis on participation and employee involvement has had two major consequences at an operational level.

First, there is a strong presumption that John Lewis Partnership managers are committed to ensuring that employees are well informed and treated fairly. Moreover, the system creates a sense of legitimacy which provides management with clear authority to act. All in all, management decision-making and motivation are likely to be good, at least so far as the intra-firm constraints are concerned. Below we examine the external discipline on managers—generally overlooked in previous research.

Second, while there is little evidence of a markedly different orientation towards work on the part of the partners, who retain a broadly *calculative* or instrumental attitude, there are good reasons to presume that employee effectiveness will be high. The sense of legitimacy referred to above, combined with the John Lewis Partnership's structure of accountability, should ensure effective handling of grievances and would tend to enhance commitment to the organizational goals, all else being equal. Moreover, partners enjoy an excellent package of material and fringe benefits, which make them the best paid in the sector. This is a powerful combination for commercial success.

7

The John Lewis Partnership and the Japanese Firm

Introduction

Recent years have seen a great deal of interest in the apparently special characteristics of the Japanese firm. In fact, the very notion of *the Japanese firm* is somewhat misleading, since Japanese corporate practices are more diverse than Western discussions often assume. Nevertheless, there is some basis in reality for the ideal type (perhaps *stereotype* would be appropriate) that has fascinated Western observers.

Clearly it is valuable for Western firms to ask what has enabled Japan, and increasingly other Asian states, to compete so effectively in world markets. But many business practitioners and academics have taken a counter-productive approach to this issue, turning their enquiries into a quest for the Holy Grail. The assumption seems to be that Western businesses can be invigorated by isolating, capturing and transplanting some secret ingredient of Japanese success, possibly with marginal modifications to fit local culture and circumstance.

Such a crusade, born of curiosity and inflamed by fear, has had practical effects; many Western firms, for example, have introduced quality circles and put greater emphasis on employee involvement. But success has remained elusive. This should hardly be surprising. The Japanese miracle is both more complex than any single cause can account for, and perhaps less mysterious than a suspicious Western public may believe (Morishima 1982). Many of the most famous features of the Japanese system, such as seniority wages and lifetime employment turn out to be: 'fairly modern inventions consciously designed by rational-minded entrepreneurs after the Russo-Japanese war (1904–5), to cope with the shortage and resulting excessive quits of skilled workers' (Aoki 1984: 4).

A much more fruitful approach is to examine the Japanese experience largely as a mirror to the practices of Western firms. It turns out that the contrast is less pronounced than might be expected. Many of the management practices and organizational principles used in the ideal type Japanese firm (hereafter the J-firm) are found in the West, both now and in the past. The study of the J-firm can become a meditative reflection on the Western ideal-type firm. In this approach, one identifies the best practices in the Western firm and asks why such practices have arisen, and how far they can be generalized. From the point of view of industrial policy, the example of a culturally familiar enterprise is likely to be most effective as a spur to action. The success of a distant and apparently alien institution can always be dismissed as due to some special factor, such as culture.

Here we identify a number of characteristics that are present to some degree in many Japanese firms that have succeeded in international markets, and that are believed to have contributed to economic performance. We then show the presence of these same characteristics, or interesting variants of them, in the John Lewis Partnership. The roots of the practice may differ, but their apparent effectiveness in quite different economic circumstances seems to justify a wider conclusion. Further investigation is therefore recommended to explore the contribution of these practices to successful business performance.

Characteristics of the J-Firm

We concentrate on three areas of particular interest: corporate finance; personnel or labour policies; and systems of remuneration. In each area we identify practices or tendencies that are characteristic of the J-firm and that have been interpreted as functionally relevant to commercial performance.

Within corporate finance we concentrate on three points. First, the balance sheet of J-firm tends to have a higher proportion of debt to equity than is typical of Western firms. In part this difference is due to particular accounting practices, such as treating accumulated non-taxable reserves as debt (Aoki 1984: 17). Nonetheless there are significant differences from the Western firm. Second, shareholders in the J-firm typically include its bankers, suppliers, customers, and other contractually related agents. Many of these holdings may be fairly small, and their symbolic effect may be more important than the direct financial liability or interest that results from this particular pattern of share ownership. It signifies a degree of mutual commitment and insurance going beyond the immediate short-run gain. Third, the movements of share prices have less influence on company decisions in the J-firm than in Western corporations. In the orthodox economic view, the share price of a publicly quoted firm, reflecting the market's best estimate of its future prospects, is the single most important indicator of economic success. In particular, a weak share price is evidence of under-performance that might lead to a take-over bid. The fear of such a bid is seen as an appropriate and necessary discipline on managers in the world of apparent separation of ownership and control.

Share prices mean rather less to the J-firm. The market is not presumed to be an infallible judge of the firm's future success. Indeed a temporary weakness of the share price would be of little concern, since share movements: 'are not thought to carry the moral pressure of an authoritative judgement of one's peers' (Dore 1987: 13). This view reflects a widespread perception that the stock market is subject to many influences that have little to do with the traditional economic account of efficiency, including practices of dubious legality. Whether one chooses to describe this as market imperfection is debatable.

The likely benefits of this pattern of corporate finance stem largely from the emphasis on the long term rather than the firm's immediate results. In contrast, many observers have suggested that the typical arrangements of corporate finance in the United States and United Kingdom tend to bias firms' decisions too much towards short-term performance, to the neglect of investment in training, research and development, and strategic positioning in markets. This bias reflects both imperfections in the capital markets and a more general failure of management accounting systems to capture the true value of these sorts of investment (Johnson and Kaplan 1987).

The J-firm also enjoys the benefits of flexibility associated with *relational contracting* between economic units in its environment, which is cemented by the interlocking of shareholdings outlined above (Dore 1987). These relationships amount to mutual insurance and a subtle form of information sharing, which theoretical models predict will break down under the pressure of distrust based on asymmetric information. In practice, the pattern of shareholding in the J-firm appears to play a significant part in overcoming these theoretical problems.

Personnel practices (or equivalently the treatment of human resources) are another important area in which the J-firm diverges from its Western counterparts. Greater emphasis is placed on maintaining a sense of fairness in dealings between managers and workers. It may well be that this characteristic of the J-firm does not arise from calculated decisions aimed at profit-maximization, but is rooted in a cultural disposition. The J-firm is also marked by a commitment to long-term employment and a secure future within the company, based on career development and a general search for the most appropriate hole for each peg. These aspects of the J-firm's personnel practices are important because they increase its productivity. Observers of Western business have reached many of the same conclusions in recent years. As Ron Dore puts it:

X-efficiency, or *production efficiency*, is as important as, and probably for explaining differences in national economic performance, more important than, allocative efficiency. ... A sense of fairness of social and economic arrangements is a crucial precondition for that kind of efficiency. ... That kind of fairness cannot be achieved in the rough and tumble which results when each actor in the market is encouraged to maximise his own short-term benefits .... It requires, instead, a good deal of personal compromise and often corporatist compromise [as well as] restraint in the use of market

power out of consideration for the interests of bargaining part-
ners/adversaries. (Dore 1987; original emphasis)

Recognition has also been growing in the West that firm-specific
human capital is often important for competitive success—an
insight that renders the bargaining positions of labour, management, and workers rather more complex than the conventional
analysis of straight conflict would predict (Aoki 1984: 24). In this
framework, personnel institutions that encourage investment in
firm-specific skills, by an appropriate combination of bonuses (see
below) and guaranteed employment, are of crucial importance.

As for the J-firm's system of remuneration, we focus here on the
practice of paying a significant and variable bonus to employees
as part of their normal annual income. Two aspects of this practice
that have interested many Western observers—the relation of the
bonus to the rate of personal savings, and its ability to reduce
unemployment (by providing wage flexibility)—will not be
considered here. Instead, we see the bonus as offering important
benefits to the individual firm, in terms of financial flexibility and
incentives. Because it is variable and of significant size, the bonus
can be used to absorb external shocks, safeguarding the firm's
performance against excessive swings. Its incentive effects are
equally important. It is well established in the contract and principal-
agent literature (Rees 1985) that output-related incentives can
encourage effort and (when the firm makes a commitment to long-
term employment) the acquisition of firm-specific knowledge and
skills. Without monitoring, however, individuals are likely to cheat
or shirk. Some institutional means is necessary to ensure that the
incentive effects are not dissipated in the strategic game of effort-
minimization.

One possible means to this end (observed in the J-firm) is social
sanctions based on ostracism, or *sending to Coventry* (Okuno 1984).
This mechanism is commonly used to enforce union members'
compliance with strikes or other industrial action (another form of
strategic free-rider problem). In the case of shirking in an output-
based bonus scheme, the effect is a continuing sanction related
to attitude and general conduct. It is also a form of constant

team monitoring, which helps to solve the problem of the non-separability of individuals' output where production is necessarily of a joint nature. Strong corporate loyalty and a commitment to collective goals reinforce the mechnism of ostracism in the J-firm. These characteristics may have arisen quite independently of the apparent gains they offer for productivity; once in use, however, they become economically rational in the sense that there are incentives to stick with them.

Some Common Characteristics

The John Lewis Partnership shares with the J-firm an ability to act without constant reference to the vagaries of share price movements. In fact, there is no outside equity, all shares being held by the Trust Company. Whilst the Partnership has issued longer-term debt, it has a very strong balance sheet and in comparison with its competitors is not highly geared (see below). The firm's financial arrangements reflect the distaste of its founder, John Spedan Lewis, for finance and the City. Maintaining control of the firm for the partners necessarily restricted the use of external equity capital and encouraged a conservative attitude towards debt, lest outsiders gain undue influence. The Partnership has always relied heavily on internal funds for its capital and investment needs.

The John Lewis Partnership's attitudes towards customers and suppliers are also reminiscent of the J-firm's relational contracting. Lewis's writings make it clear that he saw the experiment of the Partnership to be concerned, not just with the employees of the firm, but centrally with customers and even with suppliers. The constitutional directive of the Partnership enjoins the firm to consider the relations with all persons concerned with the business as important. Lewis's emphasis on fairness and participation may be rooted in a commitment to justice for its own sake, but it offered a framework for business that was independently successful.

Fairness is the manifest guiding light of the Partnership's treatment of its personnel. Lewis rejected the traditional principle that the residual value of the firm belongs to those who provide its finance capital; this shift marks the first stage of a broader conception of the role of people in the organization. While in some respects the Partnership's human resource philosophy looks back to nineteenth-century paternalistic employers of the Fry, Rowntree, and Cadbury type, it also anticipates much of the contemporary debate on motivation and employee involvement. Organizationally, Lewis's sense of justice is embodied in the principles that gains, information, and power should all be shared.

The sharing of gain is accomplished through the partnership bonus, which is directly analogous to the bonuses paid in the J-firm. Spedan Lewis believed that the bonus should be distributed only once a year, to encourage employees to save a significant part of it. Research suggests that Japanese workers save a significant portion of their bonuses; the practice of Partnership employees is not known. Information on this point would be of considerable interest in view of the continued debate about wider share ownership and profit-related pay.

The sharing of knowledge is another important aspect of justice in the John Lewis Partnership. Lewis clearly believed that better-informed employees would be more involved in the business. They would identify with it more and enjoy it more. With a better appreciation of the needs of commercial businesses, they would also be motivated to behave appropriately. The sharing of information is closely related to the sharing of power. Lewis thought of power and control almost exclusively in terms of accountability. It therefore becomes essential that partners have access to relevant information and are able to use it to question the decision-takers of the firm. Moreover, managers must be obliged to respond and justify their actions.

As compared with other large retailers, the Partnership has a relatively low proportion of part-time staff. It also appears to be characterized by longer-term employment. Given the nature of the financial benefits, together with the culture of the organization, one would expect partners to remain with the firm. Anecdotal evidence suggests that people who do not fit in with the methods and values of the John Lewis Partnership tend to move on rather than stay. These trends should produce a more committed and stable workforce than is typical in the retail sector, which has not traditionally placed much importance on loyalty. As discussed for the J-firm, such stability is likely to offer some significant benefits, notably the efficient investment of the firm in human capital. But as we show later, the increasing importance of service, training, and employee quality in competition make the whole retail strategy more people-focused.

Finally, there is the problem of free-riding in any profit-sharing system in which individual output cannot be monitored by the central authority. Once again, information is limited but there is reason to believe that the John Lewis Partnership solves this problem in ways similar to the J-firm. First, there is the strong emphasis on company identity and loyalty, engendered by the participatory mechanisms and the communications flows within the organization. This could be expected to create moral sanctions against shirking and free-riding. But it seems that there is a re-inforcing mechanism based on mutual monitoring. The Partnership system gives incentives to individuals to monitor each other's contribution to teamwork; in addition to the more usual social control method of ostracism, employees can report lack of effort or incompetence to senior staff. This approach is likely to be far more effective in a firm that is commonly owned and that distributes its profits to all partners.

With both positive and negative incentives for commitment and performance, especially at the all-important interface with the customer, it is not surprising that the John Lewis Partnership prides itself on its service.

Conclusion

It would be over-schematic to argue that the John Lewis Partnership represents the J-firm in a United Kingdom context. In many respects, however, the two institutions have found convergent solutions to common problems. Through insulation from the external financial markets, a partly contingent payment system, and a strong sense of justice, sharing, and involvement, both the J-firm and the Parternship have built competitively advantaged positions for themselves.

The next chapter focuses directly on the business principles that the John Lewis Partnership has followed since its earliest days. The organizational features that other authors have explored through the lens of industrial democracy will be examined from the point of view of running a successful business organization.

8

Partnership Principles and Business: An Analysis

Introduction

We turn now to a closer investigation of the John Lewis Partnership's commercial operations, beginning with the thinking of its founder, John Spedan Lewis. Lewis explicitly rejected the notion (the so-called equity principle) that there should be an open-ended reward to capital invested in an enterprise, whereas labour received a relatively fixed reward. This chapter relates Lewis's ideas on this point to his wider view of the world and draws connections to his theory of how to run a business successfully.

We will first examine Lewis's wider world-view as revealed in his writings and the recollections of those who knew him. This will be followed by an analysis of his rejection of the equity principle: connections will be drawn both to the fundamental debates carried on in the nineteenth century as to the proper relation between people and property, and to modern discussions of the role of share ownership in a property-owning democracy. We will then examine the application of Lewis's more general beliefs to the problem of running a business, and in conclusion we consider the importance of the retailing context for Partnership Principles.

Lewis's writings reflect a complicated view of justice. Strong ethical convictions about the nature of wealth and power compel him to emphasize justice as important of itself; at the same time, it contributes to success in running a business. Lewis's great scheme was intended to fuse these two aspects of justice by developing a framework for a company in which the ethics and the efficiency would be mutually reinforcing.

The World-view

Spendan Lewis's beliefs about management and work are rooted in his views on the relations between labour and capital. Owners of capital, in his view, should accept some upper bound to the amount they can properly expect as a reward for assuming risk. This conviction appears to have grown out of Lewis's own experience of drawing significant amounts of profit from the company while bearing little if any risk. While capital has traditionally enjoyed an open-ended right to receive excess or *windfall* profits, the compensation of employees (at least unskilled workers) is relatively fixed, even in periods of great profitability. Lewis describes the relation as one of *dishonest* broking (Lewis 1954: 165).

Lewis believed further that *unnatural* distortions of the capitalist system had led to a systemic diminution in efficiency in modern times. He was thinking in particular of the separation of capital ownership and day-to-day control of corporations, and the related perception that significant influence had passed to financiers. These observations, recorded in 1948, echo certain radical ideas about the capitalist economy of the early twentieth century, as in the work of Hilferding (1981). In his concern with the managerial consequences of separating the ownership and the management functions of capital, Lewis also has something in common with the more path-breaking writings of the inter-war period, such as Berle and Means (1932), and later writers such as Galbraith (1967). These authors share a concern with large corporations and the actual or potential problem of concentration of power. Under competitive capitalism, at least in theory, prosperity will not accrue solely to capital; instead, wages will rise. A large role for financial institutions in share ownership may bring some problems, but does not fundamentally conflict with competition or efficiency.

The role of inherited wealth has become an important issue in late twentieth-century political thought. Lewis's views on this subject are not clear.

Lewis is also concerned about inequality. *Partnership For All* makes clear his hope that Partnership Principles, if embodied in most business institutions, will lead to a classless society, defined very loosely in terms of a relative homogeneity of consumption opportunities.

Lewis' world-view is that of a pragmatic social democrat in the post-war sense. He does not acknowledge the possibility of intrinsic conflict between different economic groups and actors in society, and he explicitly hopes that a change in the characteristics of everyday work experiences will usher in a more prosperous and egalitarian society. He believed that a wide application of his ideas could help British workers become as productive as their German colleagues. In this sense he can be seen as a contributor to the exceptionally large literature on the British disease.

Rejection of the Equity Principle

The equity principle is a defining characteristic of capitalist society. It states that legitimately owned wealth can be placed in an enterprise in a form that assigns all residual financial gains, after payment for factors employed at their contractual rates, to the owner of the equity investment. This right continues in perpetuity. Conversely, if the firm should become insolvent, the equity owner is compensated only after all contractual claims are met.

This is the trade-off: risk versus reward. Common sense and expected utility theory both indicate that people will not normally accept higher risks unless the expected returns are also higher. By owning equity stakes in a number of firms, individuals can create a diversified portfolio of wealth holdings that approximates their desired balance of risk and expected return. In doing so, they supply funds needed by entrepreneurs and managers who lack capital.

Economics textbooks tell this story as a descriptive account of how savings and investment work under market capitalism. But it can easily be recast as a morality tale in which the reward is justified by reference to the risk: there is a sense of deserts involved. The self-interested actions of the wealth-holder are then seen as not only efficient, in terms of promoting the general good (i.e. a greater flow of investment), but also just, reflecting the rights of individuals to dispose of their assets as desired. This conception of property is a relatively modern one and remains controversial. The debate has shifted ground a little in the twentieth century, as the role of property has been eclipsed somewhat by the importance of political power acting directly through the state. But even today, the political debate about the correct role for the state is based on largely fundamental conceptions of the rights and duties of private wealth in the economic sphere.

Following Ryan (1984), we can distinguish two broad theories of the relation between work and ownership. The instrumental view holds that property relations are justified by their effectiveness in solving problems of scarcity and allocation, or in promoting other ends such as liberty. Work is a means to such an end. The other theory (termed by Ryan the *self-developmental view*) holds that private property is essential to the realization of human nature in work. This view, associated with the thinking of Kant and Hegel, rests on two propositions. First, that there is something intrinsically satisfying about work, which is a characteristic form of human expression. And second, that the relation between a person and what he or she owns is special and merits philosophical analysis. In this categorization, the role of alienation separates the two strands, being essential to the second theory. Instrumental positions embrace legal positivism, the belief that what is legally recognized is simply legal and that is the end of the matter. In the British tradition such questions as what is it to be an owner scarcely arise.

Two major nineteenth-century attacks on the idea of private property draw on these theories: John Stuart Mills uses the instrumental theory, Karl Marx the self-developmental view. In the first half of the twentieth century, political debate moved towards a focus on the state, which replaced the power of private property somewhat. In the last fifteen years, however, the question of the efficiency and justice of private property has come back to the centre stage of politics in the West, and in the United Kingdom in particular.

Lewis's opposition to the equity principle as the basis for an economic order began with the sense of injustice provoked by massive financial inequalities within a particular business, in his case that of Peter Jones where Lewis's salary was about equal to the employees' wage bill. This observation then became a starting point of a theory of how to motivate staff and generate a more efficient business, as well as a fairer one. The Partnership aims included raising the material rewards to partners, which required productivity increases to pay for better wages. Fairness, perhaps more than other features of the John Lewis Partnership, helped to achieve this. But Lewis's enthusiasm went further: his conception of sharing apparently extended to the sheer enjoyment of running and being involved in a business venture. Fairness as a business principle therefore arose from both financial and ethical motives.

In the last five years, business writers have laid considerable emphasis on the supposed business benefits—greater productivity and competitive advantage—to be derived from treating staff with a sense of justice. This argument has been advanced with particular force in the retail sector (see below). In this respect as in many others, Lewis was ahead of his time, even though his initial motivation was ethical.

Spedan Lewis's views on the equity principle are expressed throughout his writings. A particularly clear exposition is found in The Partnership Benefit Supplement to *The Gazette* of the John Lewis Partnership, dated 7 February 1948, which includes a message from the chairman. After laying out the meaning of profit, Lewis goes on to discuss the proper distribution of rewards:

Those, who get the profit in an ordinary business, commonly justify their taking it by arguing that it is a reasonable and proper reward for their having risked their money or their careers or both.

Up to a certain point such a reward may be fair and reasonable and, if the Socialists were able to prevent anyone from getting such rewards, they might find that people were no longer willing to take such risks and that in the end the general community was paying a terrible price for the disappearance of enterprise. But the drawback of the present state of affairs is that it sets no limit to the reward that may be taken if a particular risk turns out well (Lewis 1948).

One who luckily backs a winner and consequently receives a great deal of money would not be considered especially deserving, Lewis suggests. Although wealth is a result at least partly of cleverness or hard work, judgements of fairness depend at least partly 'on what you are going to call *reasonable*. After all, the possession of cleverness or of energy or both is itself a kind of luck' (Lewis 1948). This inevitably awkward definition is set out in the following way: 'The Partnership says that [people] should never take more than a handsome professional income, the sort of income that is enough to get very clever and very energetic people to work hard for years to qualify themselves for some profession and then to work their hardest at that profession throughout a long life' (Lewis 1948).

In answer to the orthodox charge that workers are not entitled to any share of the profit because they have not put any capital at risk, Lewis argues: 'Profit in this true, strict sense of the word does not belong as a matter of right to anybody. The economists commonly call it *windfall profit* and that is a very good name for it. Since it does not as a matter of right belong to anybody, let it be shared by all who work in the business' (Lewis 1948). Lewis then rebuts the socialist claim that his system does not go far enough, by arguing that without some material inducement, most people will not give the full effort of which they are capable, and that the 'system of partnership is simply a way of recognising and accepting these facts of human nature without going needlessly far in the direction of inequality' (Lewis 1948).

Spedan Lewis pinpoints some of the factors that were instrumental in the eventual rejection of the Fabian model of socialism, notably the problem of incentives. His realism about business efficiency, together with his emphasis on the sense of justice necessary to get the best out of people, anticipates the debate of the late 1980s. If Lewis was ahead of his time in this sense, that may be partly because the fundamental problems of running a business in a market environment do not change as much as the technology and the product do. Lewis's fundamental insight was the importance of people having a stake in their business, both as a matter of fairness and because it encourages hard work.

Lewis's ideas make a qualified appeal to the self-developmental theory of property, outlined above. He focuses on the importance of a personal link with wealth, but through the collective institution of a trust, so that the association is not so much *my* company as *our*. At the root of his system is a severe indictment of the effectiveness of private ownership if it is unconstrained by rights and duties to those who work with the capital.

In short, Lewis should be numbred among those who believe that private property is essential to economic prosperity, since state direction of resources is both inefficient on informational grounds and liable to be hijacked by minority groups. But he regards pure equity rights as morally distasteful and wasteful of human potential.

Partnership Principles

Lewis's beliefs about how best to run a business were influenced not only by the general political philosophy sketched above, but also by various ideas, largely empirically derived, about motivation and efficiency. First, he viewed security of employment and general humanity as critical factors in recruiting and retaining good staff. High pay may be effective in recruiting, but will not necessarily induce unhappy employees to stay (for example, staff turnover was high at Henry Ford's plants, although wages were relatively high). Especially if the costs of quits are significant, job security becomes an important element in the firm's way of operating, together with a humane working environment.

Lewis also regarded a sense of justice as crucial to effective teamwork performance. In effect, he called for management to be hard-headedly fair. He acknowledged that justice alone will not achieve everything; there will still be problems and grim times.

Lewis believed in the intelligent pursuit of happiness as a conscious management goal. Justice is particularly important to this pursuit.

Third, Lewis stressed the need for incentives, including material rewards. His more general ambition, however, was first to set and then progressively raise the mimimum wage; the need to provide incentives operates as a constraint on this process. There is some confusion or at least inconsistency in *Partnership For All* in this respect. Later in the book, Lewis suggests that not only are workers well paid because they are able, but quite plausibly the converse is true also (p. 167). This precursor to the efficiency wage principle (Akerlof and Yellen 1986) is not clearly defined in terms of its consequences for relative pay. Lewis may have been appealing indirectly for a basic and *decent* minimum wage, but this is less convincing. He was apparently happy to pay people high salaries if it was necessary to recruit and keep them with the firm and if they performed well, so long as the income was for work, not as a return to financial wealth.

Finally, Lewis's ideas are tinged with paternalism—a characteristic that is scarcely surprising in a thinker of his era, but potentially limits the application of Partnership Principles. For example, in discussing the partnership bonus, he suggests that infrequent, typically annual payments are desirable because they force saving among employees who might otherwise not save. The empirical validity of this point can scarcely be doubted, but the implicit compulsion is slightly inconsistent with true democracy. In principle workers might prefer to receive higher pay throughout the year and be no worse off. Clearly a genuinely democratic firm might wish to honour this preference.

The Retailing Context

The principles that Lewis held to be important in the ordering of a modern economy, and their implications for the nature of business, were quite general in scope. But the retailing sector is rather different from industry and manufacturing. Moreover this sector has changed considerably in the last ten years. Some of the changes already observed in retailing are symptomatic of the evolving economic structure of the late twentieth century. These include:

1. the focus on services, rather than goods;
2. the use of new technology;
3. the increasing flexibility of use of labour;
4. the competition for the customer's time, as a direct form of leisure activity; and
5. (embracing all of these characteristics), the emphasis on customer service.

As was discussed above, Spedan Lewis regarded his own father as devoted to the principle of customer service, although he focused on the goods range and quality rather than on the role of the staff in providing that service. The chairman and the former chairman of the John Lewis Partnership both believe that Partnership Principles, aside from any other merits, increase the 'level of customer service'. As current Chairman Peter Lewis puts it: 'It does work particularly well in retailing. It encourages smiling faces across the counter.' Conversations with John Lewis Partnership staff suggest a widespread perception among them that the level of customer service is better than elsewhere and that this is one aspect of their commercial success.

Peter Lewis's predecessor, Sir Bernard Miller, expresses the same idea in more detail: 'The retail trade is fertile ground for the Partnership system because whatever organization you've got, the man or woman behind the counter is the business to the customer on the other side of the counter ... (W)hatever he or she does is, in the eyes of the customer, what the business is doing.' This potential is then linked to the incentives that the Partnership system engenders in individual partners: 'If you can get in individuals a sense that they're working for themselves and they're behaving as a small shopkeeper would behave if his own business was at stake, then of course you've got a plus that really scores and I think this is why it's been so successful in the retail trade.' Sir Bernard goes on to suggest that the system also works well in the Partnership's non-retail areas such as manufacturing and transport, and that there is no reason in principle that it should not be applied in any business.

Conclusion

Partnership Principles are based on a number of political and ideological convictions, chiefly the belief that the equity principle of open-ended returns to capital is unfair. Although informed by moral convictions, the Partnership Principles also rest on a set of propositions about how to run a business effectively. The most important of these are concerned with treating staff fairly and maintaining a just but efficient management. These principles, putatively applicable in any area of business, are regarded as especially relevant to retailing; in the John Lewis Partnership and its predecessor, John Lewis and Company Ltd, service has been consistently regarded as crucial to commercial success.

Customer service is a key element in our hypothesis regarding the commercial success of the John Lewis Partnership:

Competitive success requires a high standard of customer service, among other conditions. This means that management have to get the best out of their human resources. The John Lewis Partnership aims to achieve this by a combination of justice and sharing, reflected in accountability of management, good pay and a bonus, and wide dissemination of information.

We now turn our attention to investigating how well the Partnership performs relative to its main competitors, in terms of conventional economic and financial criteria, and how far its business strategy differs from those of other retailing firms.

9

Theories of Business Performance and the John Lewis Partnership

Introduction

Since the 1930s, economists have developed a theory of the firm that focuses on the interactions between ownership and control. This chapter examines the implications of that theory for the performance of the John Lewis Partnership as a business.

The theory of the firm has developed considerably in the last fifteen years, building on the optimization axioms of neo-classical economics, but introducing a much broader range of relationships within the firm. In effect, the theory now peers inside the *black box* of the organization, offering a more interesting framework for the investigation of firm behaviour. The dominant predictions of the orthodox models depend on two key issues: who has effective control of the firm, and how is their behaviour constrained?

This chapter analyses the main conclusions of the literature on firm behaviour, and their bearing on the case of the John Lewis Partnership, whose most significant characteristics, from the orthodox economic perspective, would appear to be the following:

1. The firm has no outside equity traded in the capital markets.
2. The firm faces precisely the same product market as other, more conventional, firms.
3. All profits after retentions accrue to members of the firm, either as managers and workers or as partners.
4. The Partnership institutions are intended to ensure that the wishes of the workforce are considered in executive decision-making.

We first summarize the orthodox approach to managerialism. This is followed by a review of the managerialist literature about the performance of firms in which managers have discretion to pursue their own interests rather than those of shareholders. We then consider the role of take-over and the capital market in company performance before analysing the main conclusions of the literature of worker co-operatives and labour-managed firms.

The Orthodox Approach and Managerialism

The original *black box* view of the firm is a simple legal model that does not attempt to explain the existence of the firm and merely analyses input–output combinations, at a high level of abstraction. To the extent that this model has a real world counterpart, it would be a fully entrepreneurial firm, in which a single owner-manager took all decisions and owned all residual income after paying for hired factors. The enduring power of this model is that its simplicity offers concrete answers to a large number of problems which can be addressed using the conventional comparative statics approach. Its limitations are apparent, however, when it is applied to the many other questions in which the complexity of existing business organizations is relevant. The most imortant of these complications is that the entrepreneurial function can be divided into two parts (Fama and Jensen 1983).

1. The ownership function: contributing capital and reallocating it among projects, according to risk and expected return.
2. The management function: co-ordinating the inputs and deciding on how to allocate them, according to the corporate goals and conditions actually prevailing in markets and company operations.

Although there are advantages in combining the two functions, many people with managerial talent lack the capital needed to be business owners themselves; the economy as a whole benefits if they can function as manager-employees of the firm. Moreover, distributing ownership among a large number of persons, as in the joint-stock company, offers advantages of risk sharing that benefit both the individual and the economy.

The historical evolution of firms that separate *ownership* and *control* in this way has given a major impetus to the enrichment of the neo-classical model. A large literature on the effects of *managerial capitalism* examines the performance of such firms. Some authors have argued that there are limits to the discretion of managers, and that the original model may not be as wide of the mark as it seemed. The main requirement for this to be so is an efficient capital market which will discipline managers who fail to do what the owners would wish them to do. The argument runs as follows.

1. Owners (shareholders) and managers may plausibly have different objectives.
2. Managers are hired by the owners to run the firm in a way that the owners would wish; but managers may disagree with these objectives.
3. To the extent that they disagree, and have freedom to act, managers may take decisions that the owners dislike.
4. It is essentially impossible to draw up contracts between owners and managers that would solve this problem.
5. The problem is hard to identify in practice, because managers have much more detailed knowledge of the business than the owners do.
6. The firm will therefore not perform as the black box theory would predict; it may be less efficient from a societal point of view.

The first of these points assumes that managers of a firm may pursue objectives that reduce net profitability. For example, they may value larger scale for its own sake, higher wages, managerial prerequisites, and conservatism in investment decisions (Williamson 1964; Marris 1964). The owner is likely to be motivated above all by pursuits of profits. Any other considerations (e.g. ethical) can be handled by the choice of which firms to invest in.

Points two and three simply establish that managers are hired employees like any other factors of production, differentiated only in the degree of their responsibility. Given point one, there is a contractual problem in the sense that managers have to be compensated like any other factor and have an interest in taking decisions which are damaging to the owners' interests. The same problem arises with any form of labour that is hired at a wage and therefore has an incentive to work less hard or less long if possible.

It is not clear a priori just how serious the problem of managerial conflict of interest is likely to be in practice. Top managers may be quite strongly motivated to behave in an entrepreneurial manner (i.e. as if they owned the firm), even without extra incentives. Persons with such character traits could be identified partly by reputation effects in the market for managers. The efficiency of this market is therefore of some interest. The information problem is likely to be a serious obstacle here: it may be very difficult to assess the contribution of a particular manager to a corporate outcome. If the owners anticipate these difficulties, can they take offsetting actions (points four and five)? If they could identify what the managers were doing, they could sack offenders. Or they could insist on employment contracts that specified managerial duties in such details that managers would have no room for opportunistic behaviour. Partial moves in this direction include the use of incentive mechanisms related directly to performance measures, chiefly the share price.

There are two major difficulties here. The first is that cohesive shareholder action becomes increasingly difficult when ownership is widely dispersed. Since the benefits of monitoring accrue to all shareholders, each one has an incentive to hope that someone else takes on the monitoring role, with its attendant costs. Because of this free-rider problem, there is likely to be too little monitoring in practice. The second difficulty is more intrinsic. Managers function as agents of the shareholders. The fundamental problem of agency relationships is that information is imperfectly distributed (point five). It is extremely difficult for owners to know whether or not the managers' actions are taken correctly (from the owners' point of view). Yardstick comparisons may be useful, but do not distinguish the firm-specific factors that make any enterprise, in the limit, unique.

This information asymmetry creates incentives for offsetting actions. The board of directors, the annual general meeting, and the annual report all play a part in reducing information problems, although the effectiveness of such institutions is difficult to establish. In theory, spending on such devices should continue until their marginal cost is just balanced by the marginal benefit of extra profit generated by avoidance of managerial opportunism. In practice this calculation is extremely difficult, and many of the arrangements follow established custom and practice in a particular economy.

One consequence of this state of affairs is that the net worth of any firm perceived to be marked by managerial conflicts of interest will be reduced, as a firm whose managers are perceived to neglect owners' interests will be assigned a lower value by capital markets, since its profit prospects are lower.

What are the implications of the managerial view of the firm for the economy as a whole? Under the black box theory of the firm, allocative efficiency results so long as pure competition prevails; without pure competition, resources are likely to be misallocated. Managerialist views of the firm imply a redistribution of resources from owners to managers. (Once this redistribution has taken place in a given firm, however, a new owner (share purchaser) will pay a lower price, because the market recognizes that the profit opportunity has been reduced. Overall technical efficiency may suffer if inadequate monitoring encourages managers to be lazy or self-serving.

It is also possible that society will benefit from the difference between managers' and owners' objectives. The idea of the *soulful corporation*, mindful of the welfare of its employees and of its role in the wider community, depends on managers behaving differently from the classic entrepreneur. Furthermore, whereas owner-managers may take actions that reflect their own particular prejudices, whether on employment policy or other aspects of the firm's activities (Demsetz 1988), pure owners are unlikely to do so, since a much smaller part of their time is spent connected with the firm.

The net consequences of managerialism therefore depend upon a range of considerations. The general conclusion for business performance alone, considered in narrow efficiency terms, is that managerialism is detrimental.

Product and Capital Market Discipline

Even if managers pursue their own interests to the neglect of owners, their self-dealing will be limited by their desire to preserve their own jobs. Therefore, abuse of managerial discretion is likely only if two conditions are met:

1. Product market competition is mild enough that the company's inefficiency will not lead to bankruptcy.
2. There is no possibility of a new owner emerging who will evict the management.

In the 1950s and 1960s, especially in the United States, these conditions may have been met for the top few hundred corporations, as argued, for example, by Galbraith (1967). In the last decade, however, the business environment has been very different. Product market competition is intense in the manufacturing sector, as a result of growing imports from other developed countries and a gradually increasing role for less developed economies. Large firms seldom go bust, but they do slip down the rankings and can be forced to change their behaviour to avoid serious financial difficulties.

   The capital market also appears to be playing a more active role in disciplining managers. Take-over activity increased through the 1980s, partly in response to financial deregulation, and partly following changes in public policy which were less hostile to merger and take-over activity (Ravenscroft and Scherer 1987; Auerbach 1988). The logic of take-overs is that a single new owner (quite possibly another firm rather than an individual) can buy enough shares in an under-performing company to evict the managers, install a new team that will improve performance, and profit accordingly. A weak share price therefore becomes a danger to the incumbent management, since it raises the likelihood of a take-over.

The role of take-overs as a control on management is controversial. Even though this mechanism appears powerful, there are doubts about how well it works in practice. A considerable empirical literature finds little evidence of discipline in the post-merger and take-over performance of firms (Ravenscroft and Scherer 1987). Moreover, it appears to be the more profitable firms that are taken over. Share price movements do not support the argument that a fundamental improvement in performance results from mergers and take-overs. Moreover, hostile take-over activity is relatively rare in Japan and Germany, yet the long-term performance of those economies does not appear to have suffered.

Instead, a plausible counter-argument is that take-overs themselves occur for just the same reasons that have been identified as abuses of managerial discretion, chiefly a preoccupation with scale and growth (Auerbach 1988). This explanation assumes that the ultimate bidders are somehow immune from the take-over threat, which until the last decade appeared true for many very large firms. But this is not necessarily the case any longer. In the United States, the combination of lighter antitrust regulation and financial deregulation has led to considerably larger take-over bids than previously, so that now only a handful of firms can consider themselves genuinely *bid-proof*. The threat of take-over therefore looms larger in managerial perception than at any time since the Second World War; the change must be especially significant for those large firms that earlier thought themselves immune. One consequence has been that a significant number of firms has gone private, sometimes through the mechanism of management buy-outs (see e.g. Drucker 1989).

Demsetz (1988) proposes a related argument linking effective performance to a significant concentration of wealth. Taking issue with some of the empirical findings of the managerial literature, he suggests that, because of the free-rider problem, no one shareowner in a widely held firm will have sufficient incentive to monitor the actions of management; in the absence of an effective take-over mechanism, the result will be poorer performance. Appropriate incentives are restored, however, when an individual, or more commonly a family, owns a significant interest (perhaps 5 or 10 per cent) in the firm. (In absolute terms, even 5 per cent is a substantial amount if applied to a Fortune 500 firm (Cosh and Hughes 1988).) Demsetz shows that such concentration is far from uncommon and concludes that the concentration of wealth is a necessary condition for effective monitoring under capitalism. Clearly this condition is not met in the John Lewis Partnership, where ownership is dispersed and shared with future generations, in a way that current partners cannot affect. By Demsetz's argument, this arrangement ought to lead to very poor performance.

Current conditions—combining heightened product market competition and capital market efficiency (by textbook standards)—are thus largely consistent with the orthodox view of business performance. Despite the controversy surrounding the role of take-overs, the main force of discipline on managers in Western economies remains the capital market, as Jensen and Meckling (1979) maintain: 'The existence of a well-organised market in which corporate claims are continuously assessed is perhaps the single most important control mechanism affecting managerial behaviour in modern industrial economies' (p. 485). In this framework, the lack of any external shareholder and take-over discipline would be predicted to lead to inefficient performance in the John Lewis Partnership. The symptoms would be excessive managerial perquisites, poor profitability, higher costs, and poor productivity.

Employee Ownership and Performance

An accounting emphasis has coloured orthodox economists' thinking on the effects of employee ownership on business performance.[1] Although sociologists and social psychologists have suggested reasons why employee ownership might improve organizational performance, their arguments have not been integrated properly with standard economic approaches to the firm and to labour.

We concentrate here on the main conclusions that have emerged

---

[1] For a review of the debate on this issue see Bradley and Nejad (1989).

from analysis within the orthodox tradition. The discussion draws on two areas of the literature: the conventional economics literature on worker co-operatives and the critique of labour-managed firms made by Jenson and Meckling in the agency framework.

Worker Co-operatives

There exists a large body of theory relating to worker co-operatives or labour-managed firms. A major concern in this work has been to establish just what difference it makes to the standard results of neo-classical analysis if the firm is under workers', rather than capitalists', control. In effect, two textbook abstractions have been compared, neither necessarily representative of its real world counterparts. In particular, comparison has seldom been made with a capitalist firm that must bargain with a union (Elster and Moene 1989). Some of the apparent advantages of conventional firms may disappear when such factors as industrial relations are taken into account.

The literature establishes that in a short-term static environment, labour-managed firms tend to respond perversely to price changes, leading to a Pareto-inefficient allocation of labour (Ward 1958). This result comes about because in a co-operative decisions are made so as to maximize profits per head, rather than total profits. Remedies are available in the case of multi-input and multi-product firms, but there remains a strong presumption that co-operatives will be efficient.

A second important result concerns investment decisions. Older and younger workers have different time horizons. The influence of older workers tends to introduce a short-term bias, since they would rather receive company profits now and invest them in other forms (Furobotn 1976; Vanek 1970). Consequently, self-financing is unlikely to be efficient as a source of funds, and to the extent that other potential suppliers of finance (e.g. banks) are sceptical of co-operatives, there will be a tendency to under-investment. (The scepticism of financial institutions might be due to co-operatives' immunity to the threat of take-over as a disciplining measure.)

A different set of problems has been discussed in the literature on property rights. An influential argument made by Alchian and Demsetz (1972) is that when production requires teamwork and monitoring is costly, the most efficient solution is for the owner of the residual profit stream to monitor the workers' efforts. In a collectively run firm, there would be an incentive for each individual to shirk, even though the consequences would be collectively undesirable. Consequently, labour-managed firms are likely to be less efficient than their capitalist competitors, for a given technology.

This argument has been challenged at two levels. Mirrlees (1976) suggests that the Alchian and Demsetz solution to the monitoring problem is not necessarily the general one. More specifically in the context of labour-managed firms, Putterman (1984) argues that mutual monitoring may be more efficient; when an owner supervises, workers' behaviour is likely to change as soon as his or her back is turned. The idea of mutual monitoring and social ostracism as means of preventing shirking has also been suggested as a viable mechanism in the context of Japanese firms.

Rights and Production Functions

An influential article by Jensen and Meckling (1979) argues strongly that labour-managed firms are likely to be inefficient. Their argument is all the more interesting for being made within a framework that explicitly discusses issues that are normally omitted within the neo-classical analysis, such as rights and the political processes of decision-making. Jensen and Meckling employ the agency framework developed by Jensen and Meckling (1979) to assess a priori claims that the labour-managed firm will be (at least) as efficient as its capitalist twin.

Their first argument is taken from the *natural selection* view of the market economy. If labour-managed firms and German-type co-determination were efficient, then they would rise spontaneously rather than as a result of legislation. The preferences of shareholders must therefore be overridden if co-operation and participation come only through political intervention: 'The fact that this system seldom arises out of voluntary arrangements among individuals strongly suggests that codetermination or industrial democracy is less efficient than the alternatives which grow up and survive in a competitive environment (Jensen and Meckling 1979: 473).

Jensen and Meckling's second argument is the time horizon problem mentioned above: since claims in the firm are assumed to be non-tradable, current members have an incentive to maximize current net cash flow both by reducing investment and by floating long-term loans with no provision for a sinking fund. They will also have an incentive to vote themselves excessive pension rights. These incentives will in turn make the firm a very poor credit risk and compromise its financing.

The third argument is the common property problem: the co-operative will invest only in projects that offer increased net cash flow per head. As a result, it is likely to restrict membership or forego projects which in a normal firm would be viable. The upshot is a departure from Pareto-efficiency. As their fourth argument, Jenson and Meckling note that the non-transferability of ownership implies that there will be no market in corporate control. With no residual claimant, moreover, nobody has any incentive to specialize in monitoring management, as in the Alchian and Demsetz analysis (see above).

The final problem is one of control: there is no clear way of aggregating preferences in a co-operative. Pro-labour managed firm writers often assume implicitly that the members have identical preferences, but this is implausible. There is no theory of effective decision-making in these democratic circumstances, which suggests to Jensen and Meckling that decision-making will be less rather than more efficient in the co-operative or co-determined firm. How do these arguments apply to the John Lewis Partnership? The first argument, from natural selection, is persuasive but not clinching: there are important respects in which the market environment is different from the natural one (Nelson and Winter 1982). In fact, the John Lewis Partnership arose spontaneously as a worker-owned firm, albeit reflecting the preferences of only one person.

The problem of time horizons is potentially a very serious one, admitting of two possible solutions. Conceivably, co-operative members might have a strong sense of commitment to non-financial goals, including job protection and local economic development; such commitment appears to be important in the Mondragon case (Bradley and Gelb 1982). Alternatively, some form of constitution, with external legal credibility, might constrain the current generation of workers from profiting at the expenses of their successors. This is the John Lewis solution: the constitution enjoins the management to maximize the *happiness* of partners, but emphasizes that the Partnership belongs to current, past, and future partners. This constitutional injunction, combined with a strong sense of responsibility among the managers themselves, appears to meet the horizon problem.

The Partnership addresses the common property problem by ruling out partner participation in management decisions. It could be argued that managers, acting on behalf of the partners, would be reluctant to make investments that would diminish the surplus head. This tendency is counteracted by the understanding that the Partnership is intended to benefit future members as well as current ones.

Jensen and Meckling's fourth argument is perhaps the most powerful when applied to the Partnership. As dicussed earlier, the lack of capital market discipline on management would be expected to lead to poor performance in the John Lewis Partnership. Finally, the control problem is likely to be a real difficulty in co-operatives in the long run, unless they can evolve a clear and credible decision procedure. In the John Lewis Partnership, however, the whole system was imposed unilaterally from above. The emphasis on business success as paramount is enforced by the exclusion of most partners from management decision-making. In principle one might expect the system of accountability and representation to involve rank-and-file employees in crucial management decisions and therefore muddy the waters a little as compared with a conventional shareholder firm. Flanders *et al.* (1968) argued that managers were given more legitimacy in the Partnership system than in a traditional firm, and this might mean that lines of decision and strategy were clearer.

Conclusion

Two broad themes in the economic literature on corporate performance are particularly relevant to the John Lewis Partnership. First, the absence of a take-over constraint, and the lack of external monitoring of the managers' behaviour, would be expected to lead to poor performance. Despite recent disenchantment with the take-over process in the United States and the United Kingdom, the discipline of the capital market remains central to the operation of the economy in these countries. Second, whilst we have not examined the entire literature on worker co-operative and participation, the general tenor of neo-classical analysis is negative. Some specific criticisms are not entirely relevant to the John Lewis Partnership, since its workers do not participate in managerial decision-making. However, to the extent that the John Lewis Partnership shares the general characteristics of the co-operative mode of organization, the literature would predict poorer performance as measured by investment, growth, and productivity. To test these predictions, the following chapters investigate empirically how well the Partnership performs relative to its main competitors.

10

The Post-war Retailing Environment

The Economic Background to the 1949–1953 Period

Retailing was affected during the Second World War by the imposition of rationing and of course by the disruption from war damage itself, but some of the effects of the 1939–45 conflict continued well into the late 1940s. Many foodstuffs were still rationed to the end of the period we are considering, even if less severely than before. Cloth rationing formally ended in 1949 but the Utility scheme, which included controls over margins and prices, persisted until 1952. As Evely (1959) shows, manufacturers continued to allocate goods in short supply along the same supply lines as had existed pre-war. Further, outside the severely damaged cities, the building of shops was restricted. Licences were required for the modernization of existing shops where the expenditure exceeded £100: in 1952 this was raised to £500, (see e.g. Jeffreys 1955). The period was one of high rentals and inflated property prices, on top of which commercial buildings, unlike industrial property, did not qualify for taxation allowances in respect of depreciation.

The aftermath of war also brought a flush of consumer expenditure, towards durables and other household goods. Between 1949 and 1953, real spending on food and drink rose by only 6 per cent, compared with a rise of 16 per cent on durables. Spending on clothing, on the other hand, actually fell by 6 per cent over the same period, (see e.g. Abrams 1955). By 1950 the larger multiples were gaining at the expense of the smaller multiples and independent traders which had performed better immediately after the war. It was a trend that continued after 1950, but was accounted for largely by the co-operatives rather than the department stores which lost more on the decline in clothes than they gained on the increase in household goods.

The Structure of the Retail Sector 1949–1953

Table 10.1 shows the structure of retailing in 1950. Though this pattern would change over the next twenty years, the sector was dominated by independent shops in the early 1950s. Department and related types of stores accounted for under 10 per cent of total

TABLE 10.1. *Structure of the retail sector in 1950*

	No. of establishments (000)	Total sales (£000)
Independent shops	376.3	2,198
Department, variety, and other general stores	1.5	422
Co-operative societies	26.4	593
Multiple (two or more branches)	126.9	1,710
Total	531.1	4,923

Source: Census of Distribution for 1950

retail sales, through 1,500 establishments. Table 10.2 gives the distribution of *quoted* retail companies, which form a smaller subset of the total than in other industrial sectors. Evely (1959) argues that retail concerns may have tended to remain private companies (or unquoted public companies) longer than concerns of comparable size in manufacturing because of the aura of goodwill that is attached to family businesses. Moreover, retail concerns can more easily raise finance through bank loans and debentures or mortgages for retail concerns because the freehold property is generally acceptable as collateral.

TABLE 10.2. *Distribution by type of quoted retail companies*

	No. of quoted companies	Total net assets (£m)
Specialist multiples (ten or more branches)	28	50.9
Variety chains	5	45.8
Mixed distributors	4	27.2
Department stores	29	82.3
General stores	18	12.9
Total	84	219.1

Source: Census of distribution for 1950

As relatively large retailing concerns, department stores would be more likely to be quoted companies. They represent a larger share of quoted companies than retail sector overall, as a comparison of Tables 10.1 and 10.2 reveals. In all, department stores accounted for about one-third of the net assets of the quoted retail sub-sector.

A Comparison with John Lewis Partnership Data

The comparative information used here is derived from the 1959 Tew and Henderson study of company accounts for Britain from, 1949 to 1953; Evely's (1959) contribution to that volume provides some useful summary accounting measures that have been matched with data from the John Lewis Partnership accounts. Two sets of information are used here: one summarizes changes in the balance sheet, the other is a profitability measure. Table 10.3 shows changes in the balance sheet for the John Lewis Partnership side by side with comparator data for all retail quoted firms.[1] The balance sheet items are broken down into fixed assets stated net of depreciation, goodwill and trade investments, stocks, trade credit extended net of credit received, the overall liquidity position, provisions and

[1] A better comparison would have been with department stores only, but this data was not available from the Evely study.

other adjustments. Table 10.3 states changes in these stock items, and so can be regarded as recording *flows over the period*, their pattern being indicated by reporting the percentage change in the total net asset increase accounted for by each item. Evely (1959) used this method in such a way that the primary data are not recoverable; the John Lewis Partnership data are matched using the same definitions.

TABLE 10.3. *Changes in the consolidated balance sheet for John Lewis and Co. Ltd and subsidiaries and for retail quoted firms, 1949–1953*

Category	Change as % of total change in net assets	
	John Lewis Partnership	Retail quoted companies
Changes in		
Net fixed assets	83.5	17.5
Goodwill and trade investments	29.1	34.3
Stocks	− 25.9	39.9
Net trade credit extended	32.5	23.1
Improved net liquid position	9.0	6.8
Change in sundry provisions	2.5	− 8.3
Adjustments	− 30.7	− 12.5
	100.0	100.0

Table 10.3 clearly shows that the John Lewis Partnership's expansion of net assets was concentrated overwhelmingly in net fixed assets. This, Sir Bernard Miller suggests, was a result of the major war damage sustained by the Partnership, leading to a large and expensive renewal plan in the decade following the Second World War. Unlike the sector overall, the Partnership ran down its stock and improved its liquidity. Given, the financial burden of the rebuilding programme, together with the relatively poor trading profit performance (Table 10.4), keeping stocks down to the bare minimum may have been the only way to maintain liquidity. The Partnership's substantial adjustments item largely

reflects the unwinding of a number of unusual provisions and suspense accounts relating to war damage.

TABLE 10.4. *Percentage changes in gross trading profits for John Lewis and comparators, 1949–1954*

	1949–50	1950–1	1951–2	1952–3	1953–4
Retailing					
Quoted	14	9	6	19	57
All retail	4	9	−1	14	29
Department stores	6	18	−3	16	43
Manufacturing	25	20	−12	12	48
John Lewis	2	0	−62	10	15

Table 10.4 shows the changes in gross trading profits for John Lewis and its comparators in the early 1950s. Overall, retailing profitability was not as buoyant as in manufacturing, but within retailing, department stores performed relatively well. The John Lewis Partnership performed less well than department stores and also under-performed the sector as a whole. The company's poor start to the period can be attributed, in part, to the consequences and aftermath of the war. Trading profit is stated before interest and deductions, and is therefore an index of the basic ability of the company to shift goods at a reasonable margin. John Lewis's reduced availability of outlets (shops) may have worked against profitability in this period, but it is also hard to avoid the impression that there were severe problems in the basic running of the Partnership.

This lacklustre performance is of some importance considering the growth of the John Lewis Partnership later on. As Peter Lewis, the current Chairman, notes, when Spedan Lewis retired and was succeeded by Bernard Miller in 1955, the Partnership was clearly not in a good state and was not held in very high regard by its competitors. This poor profit performance over the five year period can be seen reflected in the Partnership bonus payments: no Partnership bonus was paid from 1949 to 1954 when payment resumed at a rate of 4 per cent. A special *holiday bonus* paid in 1952, amounting to a total of £36,000; this compares with a total of

£139,000 for the last Partnership bonus in 1948 which represented some 6 per cent of pay. As Sir Bernard Miller admits, this special holiday bonus was no more than a morale boost. The ability to retain profits was a major benefit to the company in the circumstances; whether a conventional firm could have survived for so long without paying dividends is questionable.

The limited comparative data indicate that the John Lewis Partnership emerged from the Second World War in a poor state financially, burdened with a major rebuilding programme. Profitability was poor, resulting in virtually no distribution to the partners for the period. Changes in the balance sheet suggest the main focus was on investing in fixed assets, principally buildings. Low profits pushed the firm into staying liquid by running stocks down at a time when the rest of the sector was doing the opposite. Overall, this was a very difficult time for the Partnership. Our study of the last twenty years was designed to test whether this was an aberration due to peculiar circumstances, or a portent of things to come.

11

A Comparative Business Analysis: 1970–1989

Introduction

We have described the distinctive features which make the John Lewis Partnership unusual. We have examined the workings of the Partnership and analysed the genesis of its business philosophy. Further, we have used the literature on business performance to understand what an orthodox analyst might expect of such an unusual firm in a commercial market environment. We concluded that because of the absence of capital market discipline on managers, the John Lewis Partnership would be expected to be relatively inefficient, with little incentive to do more than survive. Immediately after the war, we saw the company was not very profitable and appeared to be in poor commercial shape relative to its high street competitors. We now focus on the period since 1970 and analyse the comparative performance of the John Lewis Partnership and its wholly owned subsidiary Waitrose. Using accounting data and standard measures of performance, we construct indices relating to the capital structure, liquidity, profitability, and productivity of the firms as compared to their main competitors in the retail sector. These indices will show whether the 1949–53 period was unrepresentative and, more crucially, allow us to answer the important questions raised by the literature analysis.

Business Performance—Methods and Concepts

We calculate a wide set of ratios and measures relating to liquidity, gearing, profitability, and productivity for the John Lewis Partnership and for certain other firms regarded as its close competitors. Competitors are the most natural comparators to use, though this is admittedly to take a somewhat static position. Were there a continuous dynamic process of competitive growth perhaps involving diversification into other areas, then comparison only with current competitors would be too limited. Entry, however, into the department store and large supermarket sections of retailing is now very difficult indeed, largely, according to David Sainsbury, because of the major economies of scale associated with the sites, systems, and distribution networks. The structure of the sector may continue to evolve, but change in recent years has amounted largely to a reshuffling of the assets and prospects of current firms.

Data for comparator firms are taken from published company accounts, except for the Partnership's Waitrose subsidiary; its data were supplied by John Lewis itself directly for our study. Data have been adjusted for consistency and where relevant the effects of mergers and take-overs have been eliminated. For Debenhams and House of Fraser, the data series has been truncated where a merger or take-over created a discontinuity.

The companies chosen are all familiar, but it is as well to add some initial gloss to that familiarity. Debenhams plc is a department store chain regarded as a close competitor to that section of the John Lewis Partnership. It was taken over by the Burton Group in August 1985 and the data since then are not used below, since there is evidence of lack of comparability. Its turnover in 1985 was £729 million and it employed 20,000 workers. House of Fraser plc also competes with the John Lewis department stores. It was taken over and became a private company in 1985, at which time the data series ends. Turnover in 1985 was £930 million and its workforce numbered some 25,000.

Marks and Spencer plc is by reputation Britain's leading retailer. It trades in three areas: food, household goods, and clothes. In recent years it has moved into financial services, but this remains as a relatively small proportion of turnover and profits. It resembles the John Lewis Partnership in having both food and non-food areas: on the whole, however, both areas are included in a single store. Marks and Spencer does not publish separate data for the two areas other than turnover and profits—the balance sheet and profit and loss accounts are for the combined operation. The firm is therefore a competitor to both sides of the John Lewis Partnership retailing operation but cannot be disaggregated accurately. Its turnover in 1989 was £5.1 billion, and it employed 51,000 (full-time equivalent) workers.

J. Sainsbury plc dominates food retailing in Britain and is a competitor to Waitrose in the supermarket area; it is also generally regarded as setting the pace in competitive practices such as product range and use of new technology, at least in the last ten years. Its turnover in 1989 was £5.9 billion and it employed 60,000 (full-time equivalent) workers. Until recently Tesco plc was the second largest food retailer in the United Kingdom and a close competitor to Waitrose and J. Sainsbury. From a period of weak performance in the late 1970s, it has become a much stronger and more dynamic firm in the mid- to late 1980s, in 1989 having a turnover of £5 billion and employing 53,000 (full-time equivalent) workers. In the early 1990s it surpassed J. Sainsbury as the United Kingdom's largest retailer.

Disaggregated data for the John Lewis Partnership's department store business is not available. Instead, the Waitrose subsidiary is included in the consolidated profit and loss accounts, which represent a mixed retailing package. As a second-best measure, therefore, we compare the Partnership in its entirety with the department stores, House of Fraser and Debenhams, together with the mixed retail concern of Marks and Spencer. In addition we compare the subsidiary Waitrose and the two supermarket chains, Sainsbury and Tesco, which provide tough benchmarks. The study employs strictly commercial criteria, such as might be applied by disinterested external investors; the performance does not therefore relate to any index of employee satisfaction, reduced stress, or alienation and so on. The data used are all from the public domain except for certain price deflators supplied in confidence by the companies concerned.

Performance Measurement in the Retail Sector

Output and productivity measurement is notoriously more difficult for services than for tangible goods, largely because of the problematic nature of the *product*. Retailing is one of the most difficult of the service sectors to measure: the precise product is difficult to define and, in particular, the problem of quality measurement is almost insuperable. Furthermore, the retailing and wholesaling functions are very hard to distinguish, because of the high degree of vertical integration between them.

There are two dimensions to the retail product: the number of items actually sold and the depth of service that accompanies the sale. This second service element is critical and includes such things as the extent of self-service, the proximity of the shop to the customer, customer amenities, and the range and choice of goods. It is the complexity of this product which makes measurement of output so enormously difficult. As a consequence most writers fall back on some imperfect but usable index of available data. This leaves much room for interpretation and dispute.

The two most common indices used are gross sales or turnover, and value added. The former is easily available, but is only a gross output indicator. It neither takes account of the differences in firms' input costs nor does it measure the service element of different products or firms. Value added is theoretically the more correct indicator to use, corresponding as it does to net output. However, it only measure true net output if the price is not affected by any monopoly power. Retailing, especially in the department store sector, is an area of monopolistic competition, with significant branding and customer loyalty; as a result the use of value added as a measure of underlying net output is therefore likely to be distorted. More seriously, it is often difficult to calculate exactly, because of the problem of obtaining data on total labour costs, including all pension and welfare spending.

The corresponding indices of productivity are therefore sales per head, appropriately deflated, and value added per head; but there are some other possibilities for indicators of productivity. Calculating *operating expenses as a proportion of sales*, for example, offers some indication of the economies of scale enjoyed by an enterprise. *Store utilization*, the sale per square foot of store space, has also been used in some studies. A popular measure is the *gross margin*, an indicator of the conversion of goods for sale into profit. It is defined as the total revenue *less* purchases of goods for sale *less* any changes in stocks during a period, final profit being defined as the gross margin *less* wages and other operating costs.

The analysis of store utilization is of some interest but it is a somewhat superficial measure in that if store space varies in price, as it clearly does, then there is a varying incentive to use space for different types of display. Given a constrained profit problem, where space is fixed, then optimal use of space is a relevant indicator.[1] Data are not typically available in a reliable form and use of aggregated figures is unlikely to give any very detailed picture of underlying efficiency. The popularity of the gross margin measure is, as Tucker (1978) notes, due mainly to data problems. The different effects on the gross margin have been studied for the British retailing industry; the data were originally available in the *Census of Production*, beginning in 1950. Some studies explore the use of gross margins as a measure. Some people argue that it is unjust since the gross margin is heavily affected by the degree of service in the sale and the extent of vertical integration in the sector, as well as by the output mix of actual goods. Such criticisms are, however, less relevant for our study, since we are trying to make the comparison with like firms in each case; there is also a problem of data availability.

Labour productivity has been an important subject of interest for studies of retailing. Sales per head is used as an index by George (1966) who, in suggesting determinants, lists market share of multiples and co-ops versus independents, sales per shop, income per head, and average vacancies less unemployment. The deficiency of gross sales as an output measure has been mentioned; labour productivity measures generally have the difficulty that they cannot account for the role of self-service inputs between shops and of course the expenditure on other factor inputs. A model of the *use*

---

[1] Information technology permits highly sophisticated space allocation decisions to be made in shops. The aim is of course to maximize *profit* per square foot, not *sales*.

of labour in retailing has been proposed by Noteboom (1980; 1982). He postulates a linear, non-homogeneous relation between the volume of labour and the value of sales of establishments of a given type, the intercept of this relation being the minimum necessary labour to run the shop, even if nobody comes in. It is further assumed that there are two types of labour: one directly serves the customer, the other acts in a support capacity. This classification of labour may be conceptually valid, although it would be important to formulate a more precise definition of who actually serves the customer, but the availability of data is a notable problem. On the *use of floor space*, Thurik (1984) suggests a similar division into the actual selling area and the remainder, but data on the allocation of floor space are even harder to obtain than on the use of labour.

Major Influences on Retail Productivity

An authoritative recent study on the determinants of retail productivity, suggests a framework that distinguishes between structural and non-structural factors. The former category includes trade composition: food versus non-food; comparative location: urban as against rural, large as opposed to small towns; and independents or multiples. Non-structural determinants include the size of the firm, the area of the shop, the average transaction size, and the relation of productivity to shop size; and the economies of scale normally expected.

The objective of our study is to assess whether or not the John Lewis Partnership is a commercially successful company. Productivity is certainly an issue here, but mainly in so far as it indicates long-term and sustainable performance. The difficulties of measurement and definition of service output continue to force researchers to rely on imperfect indicators, especially in retailing. Data on the partitioning of labour use and space are not typically available, and the measurement of value added is also problematic. Consequently, we shall use gross sales as the key output variable; the gross margin is assessed for recent years only, again reflecting the availability of data. Otherwise, we employ a set of standard accounting measures which are applicable to all commercial concerns. These measures are flawed in a number of ways, most notably in their failure to be forward looking; however the long-time horizon of twenty years obviates this problem to a large degree.

Accounting Ratios: Background

A traditional assessment of a firm's commercial viability focuses on: its capital structure, its liquidity, and its profitability. Economic productivity is measured relative to capital and labour inputs and by use of the gross margin measure. The distribution of profits forms a final measure of importance to capital markets.

Capital Structure

A firm's inputs of capital can be sourced from equity or debt. Equity is typically cheaper in the long run, but carries the danger of outside influence and take-over. Debt conveys less outside influence, but raises the risk that in any one year the interest bill may be greater than the available surplus, possibly pushing the firm into bankruptcy. The extensive literature on the optimal choice of debt/equity ratios (Brealey and Myers (1988) is an interesting study) indicates that the optimum is likely to differ across firms, depending on the objectives of the decision-makers. In particular, managerial firms are likely to want to strike a balance between the threat of take-over and the threat of bankruptcy. The John Lewis Partnership has no outside voting (ordinary) equity at all, since the preservation of internal control has been regarded as paramount; the shareholders' funds in the operation are thus founded on the retained profits of former years. The structure of the capital of the firm can be captured in a number of ways, all basically equivalent. The measure employed here is the ratio of *total long-term debt to shareholder's funds*; total long-term debt includes debentures, preference stocks, and bank loans, all debt that is not included in current liabilities, normally one year maturity of less.

A second measure of the overall position of the balance sheet is the ratio of the firm's *fixed assets to total net assets*. This measure is meaningful only within an industry, because the importance of fixed assets varies widely across sectors. Within a single sector, this index gives some indication of both the firm's credit risk, assuming the assets are properly valued and genuinely realizable, and its commitment to long-term investment in fixed assets. Of course, this is not an unambiguously good strategy. Other long-term investments in, for example, human capital and research and development or brands may be equally or more important, though they do not typically appear on the balance sheet. In the case of the John Lewis Partnership, the emphasis would be expected to be more on people than on things and so the fixed asset ratio would be likely to be smaller than for other firms.

Liquidity

The stock measure of the firm's financial health, the analysis of the balance sheet, is normally supplemented by the flow measure of liquidity. In a sense liquidity is less critical, since a firm with a fundamentally sound balance sheet ought to be able to borrow if in short-term difficulties; but, where capital markets are imperfect, an illiquid firm may be in danger, whatever its underlying solvency. It is important therefore to assess the liquid position, and here two measures are used: the current ratio and the liquid assets ratio.

Ideally, the firm would keep its ratio of *current assets to current liabilities* as low as possible without risking a cash-flow problem that might worsen both its credit terms and its relation to customers and suppliers; innovations in financial services would make it possible to reduce the current ratio over time. In the retail sector the ratio would normally be lower than in manufacturing; in the food supermarkets sub-sector, it would be especially low, often below one.

The liquid assets measure (the ratio of current assets *minus* stocks to current liabilities) is of some interest to the retail sector, where stocks are a major component of the current assets. Improvements in stock controls and the use of better distribution systems should enable improvements in the holdings of stocks so that the current ratio should gradually converge on the liquid assets ratio. These measures give some indication of how far investments in systems and centralized distribution actually show up in the balance sheet.

Profitability

A commercial firm must make at least some minimum profit to survive. This minimum, though, is not clearly defined (it depends, for example, upon the time horizon and the extent of the firm's need for outside finance), and there is no unique definition of profit either. The index chosen here is the ratio of *pre-tax profit to net assets*. Since net assets is equivalent to shareholders' funds, this ratio measures the fundamental return that the investors are getting. In a world of rational investors and mobile capital, returns ought to be equalized, subject to the constant interference of innovations and shocks. We focus on pre-tax profit so as to avoid the occasional year-on-year distortions to profits that can result from particular tax policies and tax changes. These are relatively insignificant over the long term; the underlying performance should be captured by pre-tax profits. These are stated before extraordinary items, which alter the individual year figures but are again largely insignificant over the longer term. In the accounts of the John Lewis Partnership, pre-tax profit is normally stated after the deduction of the Partnership bonus. We therefore add the bonus back into the total to give the true surplus available for tax, dividends (i.e. bonus), and retentions. Correspondingly, for those other firms which have some form of profit-sharing, the amount spent is also added back into profits to give comparable figures. In these firms, however, the amounts are fairly trivial then compared with the substantial fraction of profits accounted for by John Lewis's Partnership bonus.[2]

[2] Our study assesses relative profitability using indices of capital to sales: labour to sales; and the gross margin which is a measure specific to the retail sector. Where appropriate data are deflated by firm-specific price indices.

Distribution Ratio

For normal firms, the distribution ratio is the proportion of pre-tax profits that is paid out to the ordinary equity holders as dividends. In the case of the John Lewis Partnership the relevant measure is the ratio of *Partnership bonus to pre-tax profits*. Any firm can choose to pay less in dividends so as to reserve funds for investment, which may or may not be rational from the shareholders' point of view, depending on whether the projects invested in are sensible, whether funds could be found from other sources, and so on; a long-term strategy of reduced dividend pay-out and profitable investment would tend to raise the share price. There is no analogous measure for the John Lewis Partnership so this choice of strategy cannot be assessed. The pressures, however, on a public firm to pay out dividends are considerable: a low pay-out strategy carries the danger of reducing the share price, if the markets cannot verify that the projects are viable ones. In the long run then we would expect, following Brealey and Myers (1988), that within a particular sector the dividend policy would not be systematically different across firms. Yet there is a well-founded argument in the employee ownership literature that a firm such as John Lewis would tend to maximize current pay-outs, because the existing workers are less interested in investing in the future. There would thus be some expectation that the John Lewis Partnership would distribute more than its high street competitors.

Business Performance—Results and Findings

Capital structure and balance sheet

Figure 11.1 shows the ratio of total *debt to shareholders' funds* for the John Lewis Partnership and corporate firms. Data for Debenhams and House of Fraser are given only up to the last year of independent ownership; thereafter the balance sheets are not regarded as consistent. Similarly, the Waitrose subsidiary of the John Lewis Partnership has a balance sheet which is not comparable with the other companies; the main item of capital is debt to the parent firm, John Lewis Partnership plc. This would give the impression of a very high gearing, but within a group of firms such a measure is not very significant.

The range of variation throughout the sector is considerable, though there is a general rise in the late 1980s, reflecting large-scale investment in technology and in new stores. Levels of borrowing for these, the most successful of the retail companies, are still relatively low on average, but in 1988 were much higher than in the previous decade.

The balance-sheet structure gives an indication of the use to which capital has been put over time, by computing the *ratio of fixed assets to total net assets*. Figure 11.2 shows the position for the John Lewis Partnership overall relative to House of Fraser. Debenhams, and Marks and Spencer.

House of Fraser is unusual in having a long-run trend towards higher fixed to net assets. All the other firms show a gradual downward trend bottoming out in the late 1980s and possibly rising thereafter, though it remains too early to be sure. The short-term increases in the early to mid-1970s for Debenhams, Marks and Spencer, and the John Lewis Partnership are probably caused in part by the effects of high inflation on the accounts: certainly, the general trend is quite pronounced. As to the John Lewis Partnership in particular, these results suggest that the Partnership overall was not significantly different in terms of its balance sheet structure; indeed, it is notable how close it appears to the trend for Marks and Spencer.

Figure 11.3 presents the same indices for the supermarket firms—Sainsbury, Tesco, and Waitrose: Here the trend is towards increasing the proportion of fixed assets on the balance sheet. This would be partly a result of the declining level of net current assets.

Whilst Waitrose follows the general pattern of the other firms quite closely, its ratio is at all times lower, even if the gap is not very large. Together Figures 11.2 and 11.3 suggest that the non-Waitrose part of the John Lewis Partnership has had a rather higher ratio of fixed to net assets than it main department and multiple store area competitors.

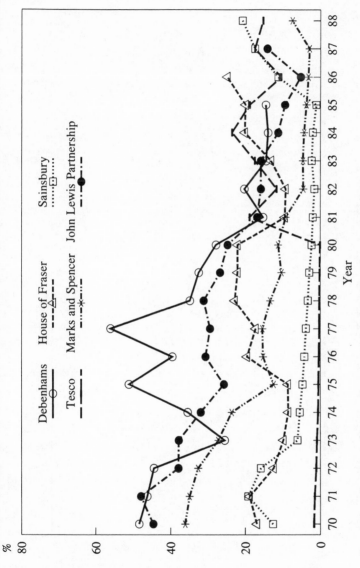

Fig. 11.1.   Gearing indicator—long-term debt: shareholders' funds, 1970–1988

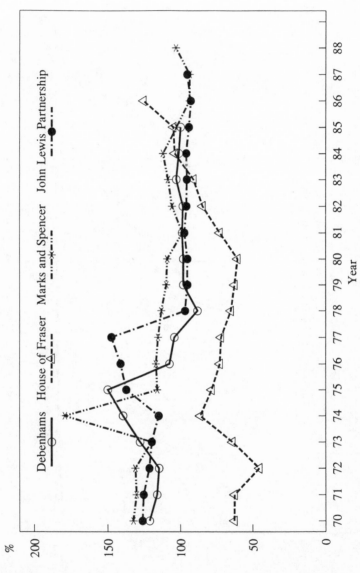

Fig. 11.2.   Balance sheet structure (1) fixed assets: net assets (non-food), 1970–1989

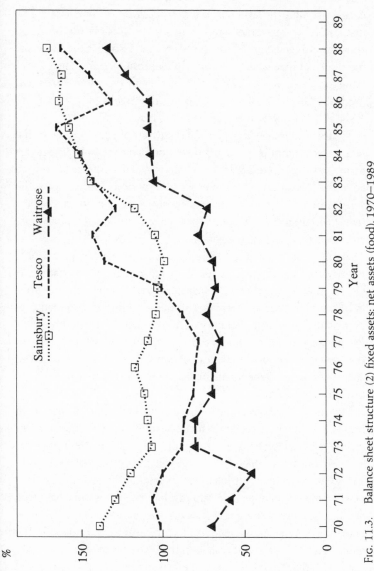

FIG. 11.3. Balance sheet structure (2) fixed assets: net assets (food), 1970–1989

Liquidity

The liquidity measures are divided into the *current ratio* and the *liquid asset ratio*, the latter excluding stocks from current assets. The first set of comparisons' shown in Figure 11.4. is for the food concerns. Over time, the measures converge so that the ratios for the three companies are very nearly identical in 1988. The current ratio for Waitrose is considerably higher in the early 1970s and gradually falls to the same point as its other two competitors. From 1984 all three companies had negative net current asses.

Figure 11.5 shows a very similar pattern of convergence in the liquid assets ratio for the same three companies with Waitrose, for many years considerably more liquid than its rivals, coming to have the lowest ratio by the end of the period. The trend for the sub-sector has been downwards in any case, almost certainly a reflection of more efficient stock control processes plus more efficient use of financial services.

Figure 11.6 compares the John Lewis Partnership as a whole with Marks and Spencer, House of Fraser, and Debenhams. As Figure 11.6 shows, there is much more variation among the firms in terms of the current ratio, and together with more evidence of cyclical behaviour in liquidity. On the whole, the John Lewis Partnership lies in the middle of the range, somewhat about Marks and Spencer but below House of Fraser; the most pronounced swings occur in Debenhams, which by 1986 had reached a very low level of liquidity.

Figure 11.7, which compares the John Lewis Partnership with Marks and Spencer, suggests that the John Lewis Partnership has on average a higher level of liquidity than Marks and Spencer, once stocks are stripped out; however, the gap is not very large and some convergence is visible at the end of the period. The John Lewis Partnership appears overall to have been a somewhat more liquid company than average over the period. There is some evidence of a declining trend in the current ratio but not so in the liquid. This is a trend not visible in the other companies, especially not for Marks and Spencer, and one that suggests gradually reduced stocks by the John Lewis Partnership over time relative to its competitors. Underlying liquidity has been maintained intact.

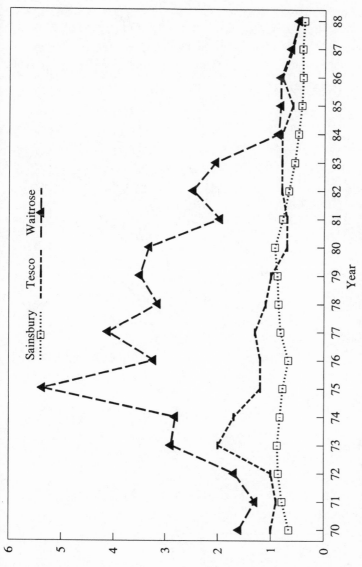

FIG. 11.4. Liquidity (1) current assets: current liabilities (food), 1970–1989

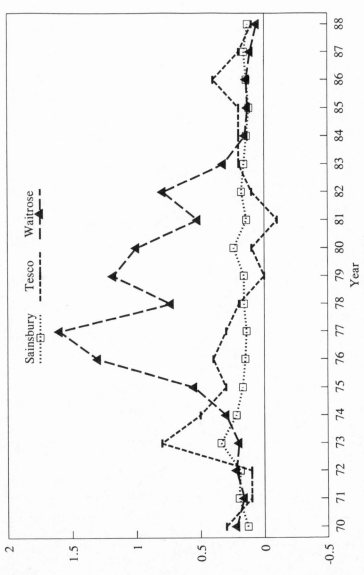

FIG. 11.5.   Liquidity (2) liquid assets: current liabilities (food), 1970–1988

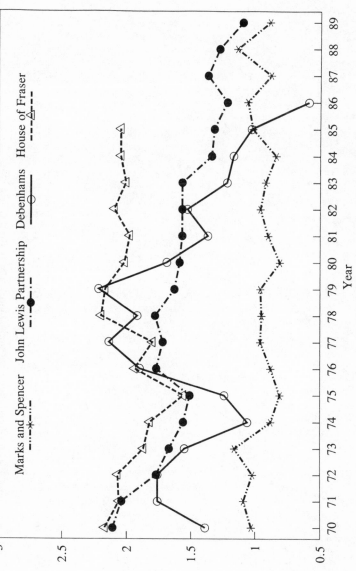

Marks and Spencer   John Lewis Partnership   Debenhams   House of Fraser

Fig. 11.6. Liquidity (3) current assets: current liabilities (non-food), 1970–1988

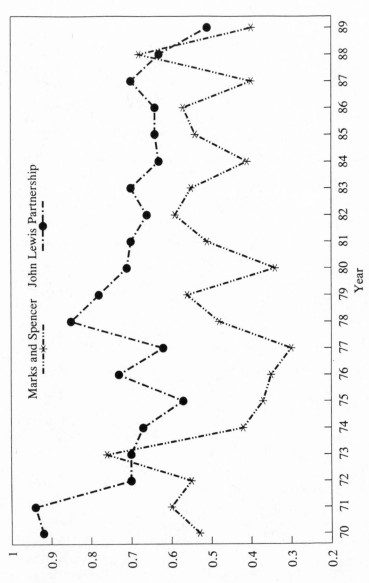

FIG. 11.7.   Liquidity (4) liquid assets: current liabilities (non-food), 1970–1988

Profitability

Profit is here defined as pre-tax profit before deduction of any profit share (or in the case of the John Lewis Partnership) bonus. The most fundamental ratio is the one which guides the allocation of capital in a market system, *profit to net assets*, or equivalently, return to shareholders' funds. This measures the basic profitability of the owners' interest in the firm. Figure 11.8 compares the John Lewis Partnership with Debenhams, Marks and Spencer, and House of Fraser.

The cyclical nature of profitability is clear, as is the wide range of rates of return among the firms. The companies appear to fall into two groups, with Marks and Spencer and the John Lewis Partnership offering higher profitability than Debenhams and House of Fraser. In virtually every year, Marks and Spencer has the highest return, but by the end of the period the gap with the John Lewis Partnership has narrowed considerably.

Figure 11.9 charts the profitability of the supermarket chains. The experience of Sainsbury and Waitrose is remarkably similar: both show a fairly steady increase in returns from the early 1970s to the late 1980s, the rate of profit virtually tripling over that period. This reflects the view of many in the sector that food retailing is no longer a very low margin, low productivity business. The decline and subsequent recovery of Tesco's rate of return reflects a complete about-turn in its business prospects—indeed, it had nearly caught up with the other two firms by the end of the 1980s. As in all, the evidence of Figures 11.8 and 11.9 suggests that the John Lewis Partnership and its Waitrose subsidiary have both produced above-average profitability over a long period.

Productivity

Given the difficulties of capturing productivity in the retail sector, the following results can be seen as at best indicative rather than conclusive. The two sets of measures given here are the output–capital ratio and the gross margin. In all cases, output is *gross* output, measured by turnover, less valued added tax where

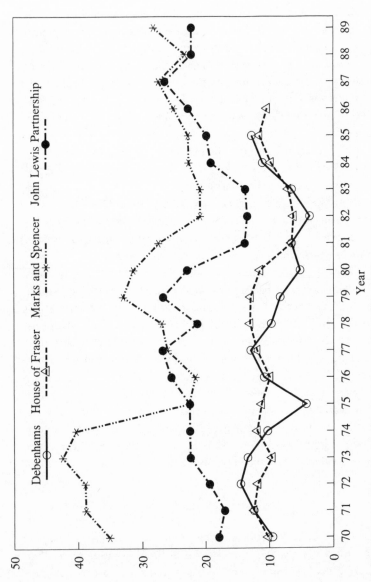

Fig. 11.8.   Pre-tax profit: net assets (non-food), 1970–1989

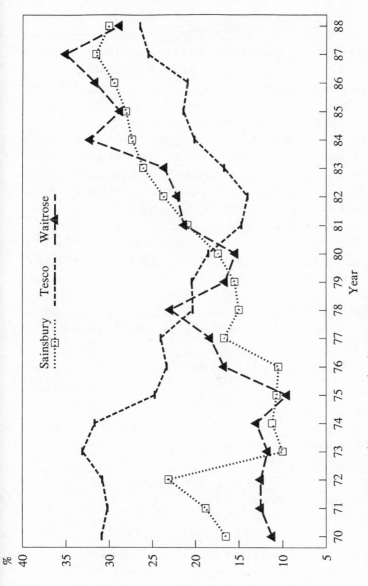

FIG. 11.9. Pre-tax profit: net assets (food), 1970–1988

relevant. Capital productivity is assessed by the ratio of *turnover to fixed assets*. Figure 11.10 shows the results for House of Fraser, Debenhams, Marks and Spencer, and John Lewis.

The uneven and cyclical nature of capital productivity is evident, probably exaggerated by the accounting figures for fixed assets in periods of very different inflation rates. Clearly, however, the John Lewis Partnership achieved a higher average output–capital ratio for most of the period, especially at the end. The gap is considerable—from 1983 to 1987 John Lewis generated about 50 per cent more turnover from a given amount of fixed assets than Marks and Spencer did and, while it is possible that a conservative Partnership's accounting policy may have kept fixed assets somewhat lower than they *should* be, the magnitude of the difference is remarkable. Figure 11.11 shows the results for the John Lewis Partnership subsidiary, Waitrose, and for Sainsbury and Tesco.

Table 11.1 summarizes some productivity data for the Partnership and its three main competitors. Although the Partnership's use of part-time workers has grown less rapidly than its main rivals, it has nevertheless achieved the highest growth of productivity of both capital and labour as measured by the compound growth rate of fixed assets and full-time labour equivalent to turnover.

Table 11.1. *Compound growth rates of productivity data, 1970–1989*

	JLP	M and S	Sainsbury	Tesco
Turnover/fixed assets	2.1	0.3	− 4.7	− 3.1
Turnover/labour	14.4	13.2	13.6	12.8
Full-time employment	2.9	0.7	3.7	5.7
Part-time employment	3.4	7.1	7.4	4.8

Note: Fixed assets and turnover quoted in nominal terms; labour measured by full-time equivalent employment.

Productivity studies in retailing have often focused on gross margin, the *ratio of profit after the cost of the goods sold, to turnover*. This measure reflects the company's ability to turn added value on its purchase of goods for subsequent sale. Figure 11.12 gives the gross margins for House of Fraser, Marks and Spencer, and the

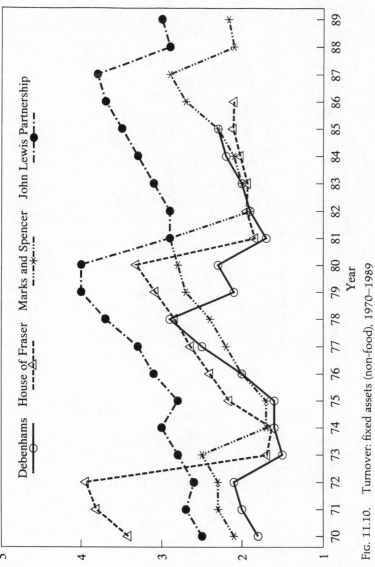

Debenhams   House of Fraser   Marks and Spencer   John Lewis Partnership

Fig. 11.10.   Turnover: fixed assets (non-food), 1970–1989

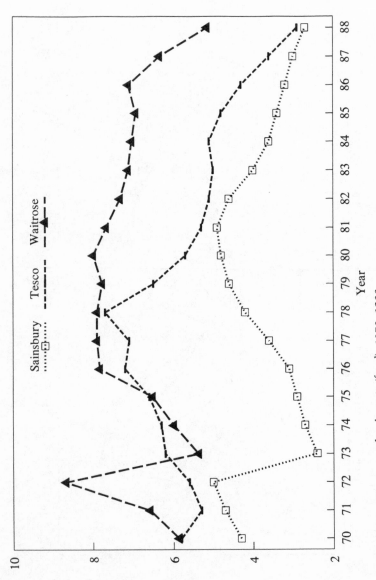

Fig. 11.11.   Turnover: fixed assets (food), 1970–1988

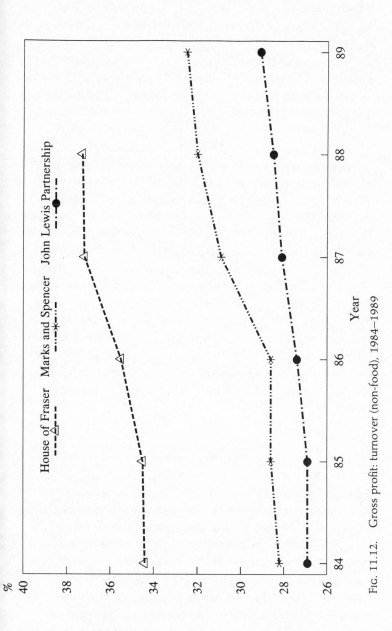

House of Fraser   Marks and Spencer   John Lewis Partnership

Fig. 11.12.   Gross profit: turnover (non-food), 1984–1989

John Lewis Partnership for the mid- to late 1980s; (the only period for which consistent data are available, Debenhams is accordingly omitted). The range is quite considerable, with House of Fraser well above both Marks and Spencer and John Lewis whose overall results are presumably dragged down by their lower margin food operations. What is interesting is how close the Marks and Spencer and John Lewis figures are.

As Figure 11.13 indicates, food retailing remains a much lower margin business, reflecting the fact that the product is more price-competitive and amenable to economies of scale that lead to high-volume low-margin business. It is striking that Waitrose achieves a much higher margin than either Sainsbury or Tesco. It is possible that the figures for Waitrose's profits are overstated. This might be for tax purposes, for example, to allocate costs as benefits in the Partnership overall; however, gross profits are stated after cost of goods sold and nothing else, which reduces the scope for allocating costs. The authors raised the issue with staff from the finance department of the Partnership, who suggested that the figures were a fairly accurate representation of the costs and revenues of Waitrose alone. However, this begs the question of incentive compatibility. Allowing then for some possible exaggeration, Figure 11.13 suggests that Waitrose achieves a consistently higher margin on their goods than do their main competitors.

Distribution Ratio

Figure 11.14 shows the distribution ratio for all six firms. For the John Lewis Partnership this is the ratio of the Partnership bonus to pre-tax profit, that is the proportion of pre-tax profit which is distributed to the partners; for the other firms, the measure is the ratio of dividends paid out to the pre-tax profit.

Two features stand out from Figure 11.4. First, the Partnership bonus has been relatively stable over the twenty year period, fluctuating considerably less than the dividend pay-outs of other firms. Second, the average pay-out in the form of bonus has tended

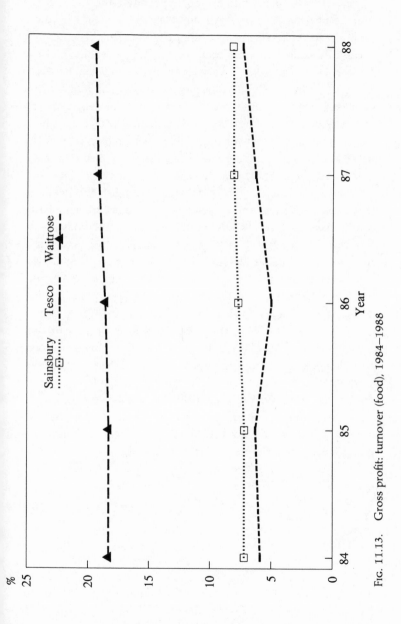

FIG. 11.13.   Gross profit: turnover (food), 1984–1988

to be relatively high, although not especially so in the last five years. Since the partners have no tradable claim on the future profits of the firm, which could capture capital gains. They do not necessarily realize a higher total return than shareholders of the ordinary firms. Indeed, it is very likely that once capital gains are added in, then the Partnership pays a smaller net return to its owners. There is therefore little evidence of an excessively short-term bias in distribution policy. It is possible also that a desire to stabilize the distribution of bonus relative to profits reflects the risk-aversion of the partners, who cannot diversify their ownership in the way that ordinary shareholders can.

Overall, the results of the ratio analysis suggest that the John Lewis Partnership and its food subsidiary, Waitrose, are not inferior to their main competitors in terms of profitability and productivity; in fact, in some respects, they emerge as better performers and rival the two market leaders, Marks and Spencer and J. Sainsbury. The Partnership has a strong balance sheet, with relatively low gearing as compared with the other main retailers, while liquidity is generally in line with other firms, whether measured by current or liquid assets ratios. The Partnership therefore emerges a stronger force than the survey of the 1949–53 period might have suggested; more importantly, it appears to refute the predictions of the conventional literature that it would be inefficient. The lack of capital market discipline on the one hand and the presence of some employee influence on decision-making on the other may be unusual, but they have not kept the Partnership from achieving a high standard of performance in the retail sector.

Findings

Our objective in examining the John Lewis Partnership as the United Kingdom's largest employee-owned company, has been to answer two questions:

1. Can a large employee-owned firm be successful as a business, given the strong a priori predictions to the contrary from the orthodox accounting and economics literature?

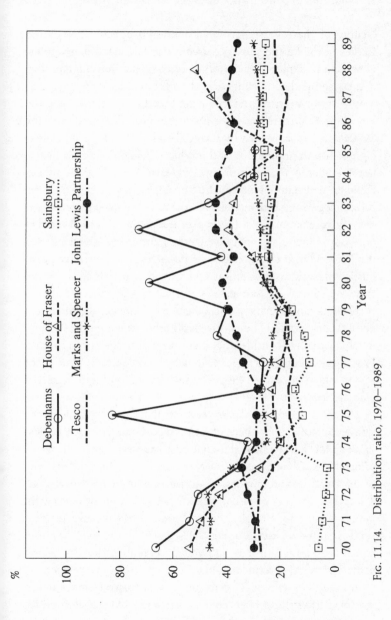

Fig. 11.14. Distribution ratio, 1970–1989

2. What role in performance does the human side play?

Neither of these issues has been addressed directly in previous studies of the Partnership. We used historical, financial, and interview data to explore the performance of the Partnership and then to analyse the determinants of that performance.

Our study suggests the following broad conclusions: First, the John Lewis Partnership was a major business success during the 1970s and 1980s, judged by financial and economic data. It ranks high or top in profitability and productivity, and shows no significant evidence of under-investment, over-borrowing or under-liquidity, which might indicate the short-term bias predicted by the orthodox performance models. The overall business performance is directly comparable with the market leaders in both the food and non-food retaiing sectors in which the Partnership operates. Thus the Partnership's experience casts doubt on the generally pessimistic conclusions of traditional performance models which imply that commercial performance is likely to suffer because of the absence of capital market discipline and the impact of employees on decision-making. The Partnership's achievement is all the more notable when we consider that it emerged from the Second World War in poor shape and performed badly relative to the retail sector as a whole in the early 1950s. The subsequent long-term recovery was exceptionally strong.

The second main conclusion suggests that the role of the human side of the business has been of major importance. From the earliest days of the Partnership, the company has been run on a set of principles which enhance financial remuneration, improve the flow of information, and emphasize service as a key commercial goal. The principles rest on a conviction that justice in dealings with people is not only ethically correct, but leads to enhanced business success. In the relatively up-market segment of the retail sector in which the Partnership has traditionally operated, this has been a successful policy, producing long-term growth and acquisition.

In the 1980s, the retail sector underwent major changes which led the Partnership's main competitors and other retailers to re-assess their approach to the human side of the business. Under pressure of demographic changes and the rapid evolution of the nature of retailing itself, the prime determinants of competitive success shifted towards a more human resource-based strategy. These changes were still in their early stages in 1989, but are likely to accelerate into the 1990s.

The changes in strategy and in institutions now being implemented by other retailers are in most respects very similar to the traditional practices of the John Lewis Partnership. These include: better training; recruitment for a more stable, long-term, and professional workforce; profit-sharing; and greater communication and emphasis on corporate culture. In sum, companies are seeking to develop a truly strategic view of the human contribution to performance. The John Lewis Partnership's long-standing success in these areas has given it a major competitive advantage, which, combined with high-quality management operating in a climate of legitimation and extensive information, has produced a highly effective business.

12

Crossing Over into the Human Dimension

Entrepreneuralism and the Role of Management

As the scale of retail concerns grows larger, and the systems and the business decisions of the sector become more sophisticated, the importance of management increases. Graduate recruitment is rising (from very low levels), and retention of key management staff is as much an issue in retailing as in other areas of business.

The traditional type of manager in retailing has been something of a generalist, reflecting a wider range of necessary basic skills than in some other businesses. It is a very unforgiving business thinks Richard Weir, Chairman of the Retail Consortium: 'You cannot be brilliant in one area and be a failure in another. You have to maintain a certain minimum threshold of competence in all areas.' Such at least is the ideal, but there is a general recognition that the management factor in the business was not always taken very seriously. A change seems to have started in the early 1980s as the expansion and restructuring of a previous rather sleepy sector demanded a higher quality of decision-making. Richard Weir sees a higher quality of management in the last eight years, and notes that the sector has had to develop its own education almost from scratch. That said, management practices before 1980s were clearly not uniform, and Weir stresses the longer established systems used in the more progressive parts of the sector. The new emphasis on information technology and systems should not obscure the continuity with the past: 'The idea that until the last five years, retailers have been *seat-of-the-pants* operators is rubbish. There has been a high level of skill in managing their inventories and in a lot of back room operations which are not very visible, but which are absolutely necessary for shops to work properly.'

The issue facing many firms in the competitive 1980s has been the extent to which overall strategy should be defined and co-ordinated in a corporate manner, with largely anonymous procedures and a bureaucratic approach, as opposed to exploiting the individual flair and entrepreneurial energy of a few key people. Richard Weir accepts that the correct balance may be difficult to achieve: 'Retailing demands a very difficult mixture of the entrepreneur and the corporate man. More so than any other industry. You can recruit people who seem to have what you are looking for and who end up being far too much of an entrepreneur.' Sir Iain MacLaurin, Chairman of Tesco plc, argues that there are limits to the seat-of-the-pants approach—the risks simply get too large: 'We are too big for the entrepreneurial style. When we are investing in a new superstore, we just can't afford to get it wrong. ... It is true that one result of new technology is deskilling. Data and control are more centralized and the business is too big for local control.'

Others echo this theme, particularly in the food side of retailing, where the need for entrepreneurship seems to be less. As John Hardman, Chairman, ASDA, points out, however, it is the judicious balance of these characteristics which is critical: 'Central planning is necessary. Otherswise there will be a lot of wasted plans that don't come to fruition. But the entrepreneurial element will always be there, in the product development. There are new fashions even in food. There is always room for new people and new ideas.' George Willoughby, Deputy Chairman, House of Fraser, sees the average buyer as effectively an entrepreneur: 'They are looking for a new idea and they are backing their judgement ... what you don't want is somebody who gets it wrong two or three seasons running.'

The entrepreneurial style embraces non-bureaucratic methods of attaining goals; it may also indicate a style of management control. Sir Simon Hornby identifies many *top-driven* firms and views the sector as fairly entrepreneurial and authoritarian. The problem, however, lies in the degree of centralization; as scale increases, many firms are searching for ways to maintain overall management control without strangling initiatives at lower levels. Sir Terence Conran stresses that goal:

Large organizations are learning something about how the entrepreneur behaves, and in lots of ways you don't only have to be good, you have to be new as well. Whilst people have learnt better how to run large organizations, those organizations won't succeed unless they manage to build-in the entrepreneurial flair on a large scale. ... The distribution systems are vital to see that the entrepreneurial activity succeeds.

The question of central versus local control has been profoundly influenced by the advent of new information technology, which in principle permits a very detailed and systematic approach to merchandising and store layout. These decisions can be taken at head office, where the data are centrally collected; by implication the area of local management discretion can be radically reduced. Chief executives are keenly aware of this tendency, and are to a degree concerned; most hope that there are countervailing tendencies which will allow local management to be more effective and use local knowledge to the full. Once again, interviewees stressed the continuity with the sector's traditional ways of organizing. John Hardman thinks that the sector has always been relatively centralized. This central control will be exercised more effectively in future, but he believes that eventually local management will have a greater say and will join in more. His historical perspective is backed up by David Sainsbury: 'I don't think that [local managers] have ever had enormous discretion. ... A lot of things are controlled from the centre and always will be because that's where you get your benefits of scale.'

Some executives see local knowledge and discretion as becoming more important, largely because local managers have access to the sort of data that cannot be picked up by the electronic point-of-sale terminal. Sir Terence Conran, for example, feels that technology will increase managerial discretion at the local level: 'Stores of the future will be much more representative of their locality because the information is there to allow you to do that. The technology now gives us the opportunity to fine tune the location to the benefit of staff and consumers.' Richard Weir agrees: 'Any retailer worth his salt would want to know how much space is devoted in a particular high street to a particular category, to know whether you are competitive and making the maximum use of the potential in that particular location and therefore tapping into local management knowledge.'

Significantly, however, it is the management of people that most chief executives regard as the most important future role of local managers. Although the John Lewis Partnership reflects a considerable degree of accountability-based democracy, it is a relatively autocratic organization in terms of its day-to-day management. The chairman has considerable power to make policy and implement it, subject to the ultimate constraint of the Central Council. Thus the John Lewis Partnership would appear to be closer to the more centralized model of retailing organization than its participatory nature might at first suggest.

As we have seen, sites and technology remained important strategic issues in retailing in the late 1980s, at least in the sense that competitive success required firms to get these factors right. However, in these areas it is difficult for the leading retailers to distinguish themselves by doing better than their competitors. The new area of competition lies in the human dimension.

Demographic changes are altering labour supply, with an adverse impact on retailers; technology and new systems have increased the need for higher quality of labour; and a new emphasis on the competitive role of service is pushing retailers towards a more professional, stable workforce. In response to these pressures, retailers are altering their attitudes and refocusing attention on recruitment, training, remuneration, and motivation. Some firms are aiming to reduce their use of people altogether, others are placing their main emphasis on competing through the quality of staff. These various approaches require a different relationship between workers and management and thus have implications both for pay and for company culture.

The Context: Changes in Labour Supply and Demand

A combination of external forces is changing the management of human resources in the retail sector. One factor in the 1980s was the growth of competition in the sector, amid restructuring and the wider availability of finance for expansion and take-overs. At the same time, new technology has become more important, especially electronic point-of-sale equipment, which is increasingly networked into a complete centralized distribution and stocking system. Finally, demographic forces have impinged on labour supply, reducing the number of available younger workers, on whom retailing has traditionally relied, and making graduate labour more scarce just when retailing's need of skilled management is increasing.

At the level of management, these external forces are generating a need for better quality decision-makers in retailing, managers capable of handling more information and potentially very risky investment projects. The scale of modern retailing is now very large, putting significant pressure on management skills. At the shop-floor level, greater competition manifests itself in a need to keep the customer happy, and a corresponding focus on the experience of shopping. The relevant factors include not only the quality and price of the merchandise, but the design, the ambience, and even, as the Managing Director of Body Shop, Anita Roddick suggests, the smell of the shop. Above all, the shopping experience depends on the nature of the interaction with the people working in the store.

More than in the past, therefore, the success of a retail business depends on the shop-floor staff. This is partly a matter of manner and approach, but information, competence, and authority are also involved. The individual serving the customer becomes a complex, uncertain, and strategic element of the firm's competitive success. This view of the employee, now gaining currency among many retailers, is a long-established perspective of the John Lewis Partnership.

Recruitment and Training

Retail decision-makers have already begun to respond to demo-graphic and competitive pressures as they affect the supply of younger workers and the need for higher quality management trainees. In both cases the difficulties of recruitment and turnover have implications for the role of training.

The Younger Workers' Problem

Richard Weir, Director, Retail Consortium, is concerned that increased competition for graduates may keep the retail industry from recruiting the best. Further, the sector may lose its skilled graduates.

Retailing has traditionally relied on younger workers at the sales assistant level, for it has needed flexible and cheap labour, not necessarily of high quality. Even as the quality constraint increases, the need for flexibility has kept younger workers at the centre of basic recruitment. As Garfield Davies, General Secretary, USDAW, points out, these workers have disproportionately been female. In future the competition for these workers will increase substantially, as will their cost, because of demographic changes in the labour force. As the baby-boom generation moves on, there is forecast to be a drop of around one-quarter in the teenage workforce by the mid-1990s, which will severely affect businesses that rely on such workers.[1] One such business is retailing, which will find itself in particular competition with, for example, the National Health Service for young female labour.

In the past, young recruits have often remained with a retail firm for a longer-term career. Indeed, the schoolboy and schoolgirl entry port to the firm has been an important part of the traditional recruitment of the more stable part of the workforce. Given that pay and conditions are generally less favourable in retailing than in other sectors, there is likely to be a fairly rapid rise in wage costs

[1] *Young People and the Labour Market, a Challenge for the 1990s*, National Economic Development Office (1988).

for young labour and pressure for better conditions of employment. Retail firms thus face three possible choices, not mutually exclusive: pay more as required and compete for the declining pool of labour; shift to employing other types of labour; or reduce their use of labour overall.

According to Roger Saoul, head of Economic Information, Marks and Spencer, only about half of the many young people recruited into retailing remain for the long term: 'There is tremendous wastage, largely because retailing is and always will be for the ordinary shop assistant not a particularly attractive job in terms of physical demands made.' Richard Weir also recognizes that difficulties lie ahead: 'The shortage of young people is already beginning to hit the recruitment policies. No one seems to know exactly how to deal with this.'

Many retailers have begun to increase pay in an attempt to improve retention. (Teenage workers are likely to care more about basic cash remuneration than other benefits.) Allowances have been raised, London weighting areas have been extended and there have been rises in maternity pay and leave. The Boots Company plc introduced term-time job contracts for some working mothers in 1989, and Dixon Group plc offer a similar scheme. Early in 1989 Tesco plc offered a 22 per cent pay increase to younger workers and extended holiday benefits to part-timers. Most other large firms have followed suit.

Working conditions are more difficult to change, however. The flexibility that retailers value in younger workers amounts to a willingness to work unsociable hours for which other workers would demand greater compensation. Thus a strategy of competing harder for young workers is likely to result in a steeply increased wage bill for retailers.

There is a growing consensus that better pay alone will not be enough to attract and retain younger staff in the future. With this in mind some employers are focusing on the nature of the work itself. Anita Roddick observes:

The education of the staff is a cornerstone. It's why people stay. There's great competition to get staff . . . we tend to place enormous emphasis on the people themselves rather than their academic qualifications. The big fear, in central London is that nobody wants to work there. So you have to have the carrot of pay, but once you've got the pay it's no longer a carrot. [So] you educate and develop people.

David Sainsbury also foresees an emphasis on career development: 'I think that the demand on young people will be so intense that we will have to say, "we can offer you this kind of development, this kind of career." I think we already do this in a big way, but that will be increasing. In the future we will put a lot of emphasis in bringing women back into the workforce after they have had a baby.' Sir Iain Maclaurin outlines the Tesco solution: 'Changes in recruitment have reflected the problem of supply. We have more mature people now. We do more direct recruiting at schools and have more use of employment incentives. This does drive up costs, but also creates pressure to reduce costs elsewhere.' Retailers are painfully aware of the cost implications of the recruitment problem. Richard Weir points to a 'tremendous tension' between efforts to control costs and 'having a skilled, highly dedicated staff, which is tremendously important in the long run. . . . How this [tension] will be resolved I am not sure.'

A second possible strategy, already adopted by some retailers, is to employ more older people. They have employed married women to a degree in the past, and may now have to increase their reliance on these workers. There is also a large potential pool of significantly older workers, in the form of retired people or those about to retire. Such workers may be less flexible than their younger counterparts, but may be workable substitutes in other respects. In effect, retailers can raise the supply of labour by using special recruitment techniques and by changing perceptions of traditional practices; this strategy will help to restrain the rise in wage costs. Roger Saoul sees another benefit in using older workers: 'There is a broad principle in retailing that you try to get staff who relate to your customers. As the population ages, my guess is that retailers will try to recruit people from the age groups they are serving.'

There may be some limitations on retailers' ability to substitute older workers for the traditional younger workers. As David Sainsbury points out, retailers use part-time workers not just because they come cheap, but in order to 'schedule the labour when you want it within the week'. It remains to be seen whether older people will be willing to work such part-time schedules. Such a strategy will also depend on the nature of the firm, Sir Terence Conran believes: 'It's a bit more difficult if you are Burton's because I don't think having a 55-year-old woman sitting in Burton's would quite work. But I don't think that is quite so obviously true of Mothercare or British Home Stores.[2]

The third strategy for retailers—reducing their overall use of labour—is more radical and could conflict with other objectives of policy, notably the intention to deliver better service to the customer. As labour becomes more expensive, one would expect employers to substitute capital where possible, which might mean a quite different style of retailing. 'Fewer shop assistants are likely' in the future according to Sir Simon Hornby. 'There will be a shortage of retail staff as they will become more expensive. We will have to manage with fewer people.'

Given this overall recruitment problem, how would the John Lewis Partnership, with its particular organizational structure, be expected to fare relative to its competitors? To address this question, we might begin with the finding of Bradley and Estrin (1987) that labour turnover in the Partnership is considerably lower than the sector norm which suggests an advantaged position. Moreover, because Partnership wages are relatively high (which may of course be a major reason for the lower turnover), overall sector wage inflation should not put immediate pressure on the company. Third, the Partnership has relied less on part-time labour than its main competitors anyway and may be able to adjust to a regime of scarcer labour more easily. In sum, the Partnership is well positioned to cope with many of the coming changes.

---

[2] In the 1980s, under the chairmanship of Sir Ralph Halpern, Burtons was transformed from a traditional menswear store to appeal to a much younger, design-conscious market.

Management Trainees

As the retailing sector has become a more complex and fast moving sector, its need for higher quality managerial labour has grown, and graduate recruitment has increased substantially. Graduates have begun to find the sector more attractive, reflecting the greater dynamism and scale of the business within it, according to David Sainsbury.

Retailing has not been attractive for a very long time. It didn't attract people of very high calibre. Retailing has changed in terms of its glamour. Firstly it has become very profitable, and also it has become very much more interesting because of having total control over your destiny. You decide not only on where the shop will be, what it will look like, how you will train your staff and how you will advertise your services, but also what the product will be, how it will be designed, and how it will be made and where it will be made. So retailing has actually ended up controlling manufacturing.

Larger retailers in particular are coming to depend on managers with strong analytical skills, able not only to process the increasing amounts of information available but to plan for longer-time horizons in conditions of considerable uncertainty. In this respect, John Lewis stands out as well ahead of the field. As the firm's former Chairman, Sir Bernard Miller notes, the Partnership has been recruiting graduates for thirty years or more and has had a policy of periodically searching for high-quality decision-makers. The annual reports over the years indicate that a large proportion of these managerial recruits have been ex-civil servants. More generally, the Partnership has cast its net wider than have its competitors in recruiting decision-makers, going well beyond the retail sector itself.

The growing demand for graduates in retailing may not be easily satisfied, since they have historically gravitated towards other sectors. There is, though, a feeling that retailing is now becoming sufficiently attractive to graduates that recruiting may not present too serious a problem. As Sir Simon Hornby said: 'We are recruiting more graduates into the industry than we ever did.

If you go back fifteen years graduates didn't think about retailing, but now it is fairly popular, which will give us a better calibre of candidate.' Similarly, while acknowledging that retailing has not been a preferred career for graduates, Richard Weir emphasizes the opportunities in the sector:

Retailing ... has a number of major advantages, including obtaining considerable independence and responsibility at an early age. This is also the case in the least favoured parts of retailing, such as managing a branch. Although [branch managers] are of course tightly controlled by head office, they have a great deal of discretion. If retailers ever became desperately short of recruits, they could always advertise in terms of giving young people opportunities at a remarkably early age.

This change in the perceived attractiveness of retailing for graduates parallels the overall change in the role of management in the industry, which is linked in turn to the scale of operations and their increasing sophistication.

Retailing is not the only sector to have found its appetite for graduate labour increasing. According to Pearson and Pike (1989) the demand for university graduates over the 1990s is expected to rise by about 3 per cent annually. The supply of graduates is expected to rise at a rate of only 1.3 per cent for the next two years and thereafter to fall. To compete in the struggle for scarce graduate labour, retailing is likely to offer better pay and conditions, especially with respect to career development. In addition, the sector may train non-graduates to perform some tasks currently reserved for graduates. In a sense, this trend amounts to a reversion to former practice in retailing, but at a much higher level of commitment in terms of training.

Some would argue that managers need not necessarily be graduates. Sir Simon Hornby, for example, suggests that 'running a shop doesn't need be done by a graduate. That's not a critical factor.' Most retailers, however, continue to look to graduates for potential managers. 'Our managerial recruitment is essentially a long-term problem; it's acute even now', said Roger Saoul. 'We are strengthening the retail image in further and higher education', he added.

David Sainsbury, whose firm makes a considerable effort to visit universities, and talk with graduates, finds evidence of favourable changes in graduate preconceptions. Formerly, he explains, retailing was at the bottom of the list in graduates' employment preferences:

Top was the civil service, [then] City and probably the professions, and last of all manufacturing. Then last, last, last, retailing. Today ... I think industry generally is viewed more favourably by graduates. Within that I think the retail industry is seen to be quite an exciting and interesting place in which the United Kingdom does rather well. ... Yes it's become a more skilled and difficult job but then by that very nature it's becoming rather more interesting.

Many firms express a fairly optimistic view that retailing has become more attractive for graduates. In particular, David Sainsbury stresses the degree of responsibility that a graduate trainee should expect: 'If you are an undergraduate and you can see yourself by your early 30s running a modern computerized store with three or four hundred people, doing a substantial turn-over ... that's quite an attractive proposition.' Such prospects should ease the recruitment problem. In this respect, says Denise Taylor, Executive Assistant at the National Retail Training Council, the last twenty years have seen 'quite a revolution. I think graduates now see all sorts of exciting things happening within the industry and there are so many opportunities. It almost doesn't matter what you studied.'

The problem of graduate recruitment is one that is at least familiar to the John Lewis Partnership, and its greater experience may be of some value in competition with other firms. More significant, though, is the Partnership's long-standing commitment to training for managers, combined with a well-defined career path. The pay package, including the bonus, is highly competitive within the sector. While the bonus has always been mentioned in job advertisements, specific figures were not cited until early 1989. Now average bonus figures over the last five years are quoted—suggesting the need to demonstrate just how significant the financial value is.

To obtain a better understanding of these employee issues, we investigated the Partnership's public face in the labour market. Several researchers were asked to apply for sales assistant and management trainee jobs in different high street stores in given geographical locations. From their findings we were able to construct a picture of how the John Lewis Partnership presents itself to potential employees relative to other high street retailers. The shops were grouped into three categories for the purpose of reporting: (i) *Majors* (Marks and Spencer plc, GUS, Safeway plc, Selfridges, The Boots Company plc, Barkers, Debenhams, D. H. Evans, and British Home Stores); (ii) *Minors* (smaller specialized chains such as Next, Thorntons, Benetton, Paperchase, and Coles); and (iii) *Locals* (small-scale shops such as tobacconists, chemists, electrical shops, and small boutiques).

The John Lewis Partnership pays it sales assistants well by the standards of the retail sector, even before the bonus and other benefits have been taken into account (Table 12.1). In 1987 a weekly income for check-out staff in the John Lewis Partnership amounted to £110.40 as against £105.00 for comparable work in the *Majors*, £104 in the *Minors*, and £105 for *Locals*. Although some shops undertaking rapid expansion offered a slightly higher hourly rate, the Partnership's basic pay was virtually the highest on offer. The bonuses, 24 per cent of basic pay in 1987, raised total renumeration in the Partnership to well above the level on offer elsewhere in the high street. Further, the John Lewis Partnership compared extremely favourably in terms of conditions, hours of work, welfare benefits, and so on.

The survey for management trainees was necessarily more limited because few of the minors and none of the locals operated such schemes. Even among the majors, moreover, some personnel departments were either ignorant of the company's management training scheme, or cut off discussion because no openings were currently available. In general, the manner in which these facts were explained did not leave our researchers with a favourable impression of the organizations involved. Table 12.2 accordingly reports on three major companies only: the John Lewis Partnership, Marks and Spencer, and the House of Fraser (a comparable company to the John Lewis Partnership, for which we did not have a long

TABLE 12.1. *Relative pay and conditions for sales assistants in 1987*

	Average majors	Average minors	Average locals	John Lewis
Pay per hour (£)	3.00	2.60	2.50	3.20
Hours per day	7.00	7.00	7.00	5.75
Pay per week (£)	105	104	105	110.4
Bonuses	Rare and small (max. = 4% basic pay)	None	None	20% of basic pay (average 1970–87), 24% in 1987
Staff discount (%)	15	15	–	10 rising to 20 after 3 years
Subsidized meals	Sometimes	No	No	Yes
Paid holidays	Usually 3 weeks	Usually 3 weeks, often only after 1 year employment	Usually 3 weeks, often only after 1 year employment	Usually not specified
Sick pay	Yes	After certain period of employment	Usually after certain period of employment	Not specified

series of economic data). From the perspective of our researchers, these three companies displayed easily the most attractive approach to personnel management.

Even among this élite group of high street retailers, the John Lewis Partnership comes out very well with regard to management training. For a person with the right qualifications, their pay is the best, even excluding the large bonus. Career structure, participation, and training are well worked out. The only company in our survey that operated at a comparable level was Marks and Spencer, another highly successful firm with a strongly paternalistic ethic.

In speaking with prospective managerial trainees, recruiters at the John Lewis Partnership drew attention to the company's unusual ownership and participatory structure, and emphasized that managers needed to be able to operate effectively within a

TABLE 12.2. *Relative pay and conditions for management trainees in 1987*

	Marks and Spencer	House of Fraser	John Lewis
Pay (£)	9,500	6,500	8,000–10,000 depending on experience, age, and academic qualification
Profit-sharing	Yes, based on profits earned and linked to basic wage. Equal to 4% wage in 1987	Existing schemes scrapped after acquisition	Yes, 24% of basic wages in 1987
Career structure	Store-based ladder	Department-based, store-based ladder	Department and ladder
Perks	Annual bonus, medical insurance, non-contributory transferable pension scheme, 20% discount	Not explained	Subsidized food, 10% discount for first years rising to 20% after 3 years
Participation	Each employee has personnel manager, weekly advisory departmental meetings	Not mentioned	Branch councillors, committees for communication, central councillors
Training	Usually in-house and well specified depending on sector	1–2 weeks formal training, not in-house. Then in-house and specific	Usually in-house and well specified depending on sector

participative environment. As for sales assistants, the company laid down employee rights to profit-sharing, participation, and information. Thus the experience of our researchers suggests that the John Lewis Partnership management is probably self-selected to work well in a relatively democratic organizational structure.

Because the John Lewis Partnership stresses the specific characteristics of the firm from the outset, employees who accept a job there might be expected to be particularly likely to integrate with the unusual organizational culture. Such self-selection may be reflected in the Partnership's rate of labour turnover, which is very low for a retail firm. In the first six months of 1970–1, a time of full employment in the economy as a whole, only some 17.5 per cent of employees (including part-timers) left the firm. By 1984–5 the figure had fallen to 7.1 per cent (again in the first half year), reflecting perhaps the slacker labour market. Labour turnover rates in the retail sector as a whole are typically far higher, often in excess of 30 per cent per annum, though we have no specific information about comparators. Overall, the Partnership's approach to the labour market seems to have put it in the position to choose the best workers, in very much the manner suggested by efficiency wage theories.

Training

Over the years, training has not played a very important role in most retail organizations. With labour costs a major variable element in the cost structure, training has been seen as an expense to be minimized, particularly given the relatively high turnover rate prevailing in the sector. Training did not seem important to competitiveness, except in those relatively few shops that emphasized service above all else. Other retailers focused more on keeping prices low. Now this traditional pattern is changing, although only slowly. As retailers introduce new technology and reorient their strategies to customer service, they are putting more emphasis on training, which in turn leads to a new concern with turnover and other personnel objectives. As John Hardman points out: 'In 1979 staff training was minimal and there was little management development. It was a culturally unattractive industry and few graduates entered. Now we spend much more money on training and this is likely to continue. It leads to a need for reduced turnover, to reduce the lost costs of training. In future we want to move to a higher pay and fewer people workforce.' Richard Weir sees an enormously wide variety of responses to this problem:

The best retailers offer intensive and adequate training and retraining. In many retailers, particularly some which have expanded very rapidly because of a formula which turned out to be successful, training frankly is neglected. This has been possible because the labour market has been a buyers' rather than a sellers' market. That of course is changing. Getting staff is now a real problem. There is incredible divergence between the best and the worst and a lot of quite big companies in the middle whose standards fall well short of those of the best.

Denise Taylor from the National Retail Training Council sees the problem in broader terms: 'Management training may well be much more advanced. But management represent only a small proportion of the people who work in the industry and our concern begins with the large number of people because there is a requirement to train employees at all levels.'

Some retailers have always placed more emphasis on training, notably those whose customers are relatively discriminating. Among larger retailers, the John Lewis Partnership has been relatively unusual in taking training seriously, motivated by a strong customer-service orientation. Furthermore, the desire of Spedan Lewis, the Partnership's founder, to share the *fun* of running a business introduced, in the view of its last two chairmen, a strong pro-training attitude to the company.

The introduction of new technology and systems brought new training needs in the late 1980s. In the longer term, these systems may be associated with deskilling; more immediately, however, staff at the check-out or service-counter level need to be introduced to the new technology. In addition, technical changes in ordering, warehousing, and distribution all require retraining for a large number of staff. Marks and Spencer, as Roger Saoul points out, train for two things: 'to give service to the customer and to use the new systems properly'. Training for the new technology was non-existent until five or six years ago, according to Sir Iain Maclaurin. Now, however, 'it's crucial and everybody does it.'

At higher levels, there is a need for training the managerial personnel who have to work with the new systems. Such training may be quite detailed and complex in scope, requiring a significant investment in firm-specific systems knowledge. This, as David Sainsbury recognizes, can lead to non-financial costs: 'The transition [to working with computers] was very difficult for managers who'd grown up in the service store and were 45 or 50 when it became a self-service store. There were a lot of people who couldn't make that transition at a management level. For people who have grown up in self-service it's a gradual process, in which you are adding on more complicated systems.' Equally, he recognizes, there are intrinsic and indirect benefits to training for the new technology:

At the very junior end of employees, there has been a tremendous response to being trained—on store computers and most recently on the laser check-outs. I think that the whole of that technology has given branch management some discretion. They don't have discretion in the sense that they can decide what the prices are going to be, or whether they are going to stock a particular product or not, but it has allowed them to manage more closely what happens in their store.

A second, and perhaps more fundamental, motivation for training in retailing is the growing importance of customer service. For some retailers, success depends critically on having staff who are well informed about the firm and its products. Says Anita Roddick: 'The key to it is training. We train for knowledge, so there's nobody on hard sell in our shops. Just people who know about the product.'

Employees may also be trained for customer service. Some retailers use customer awareness programmes, which try to show the staff how important the customer's perception is for competitive success. Actual training schemes range widely—from exhortations to smile to the use of videos that focus on the dynamics of personal encounters, with the goal of helping staff avoid antagonizing the customer. At ASDA, John Hardman sees such training in the context of the corporate objective to provide service:

We have been training to develop employee attitudes and customer service training. This stems from the corporate objective to provide service, which we reinforce by specific training and showing

employees how they can deal with customers more politely, effectively, and so on ... We also have a customer care campaign,
although there is the danger that they become flavour of the month.
We emphasize how to deal with irate customers for example. We
train every individual.

It is not altogether clear that these training programmes are
properly thought out, or that they actually work. Indeed, under
some circumstances they run a severe risk of antagonizing the
staff themselves, which is wholly counter-productive. Sector-level
training was codified in 1989 in a new *Retail Training Certificate*,
developed by the National Retail Training Council, under the
framework devised by the National Council for Vocational Qualifications. Its content, however, has been strongly criticized: in
particular, Prais and Jarvis (1989) see it as being too narrowly job-
specific and likely to lead to 'a section of the workforce inhibited
in job-flexibility and inhibited in the possibilities of progression'.

It is part of the John Lewis Partnership's reputation that their
staff are unusually well trained with respect to product knowledge.
This is a crucial element in a customer-focused strategy that
assumes the (potential) buyer is not sure what he or she wants.
Such a customer will presumably value the service of an employee
who does not recommend the product that offers the highest
commission. The role of the bonus, backed by the Partnership
institutions that emphasize corporate identity, should encourage
staff to make a successful long-term relationship with customers,
rather than go for the quickest profit. Increasingly, the worth of
such long-term relationships is being recognized, as retailers see
that customers are not just individuals who make purchases, but
can function as highly credible sales representatives among their
friends and co-workers. If one satisfied customer will generate (let
us say) five more, it becomes that much more sensible and necessary
for the seller to ensure that every customer he serves will go away
happy.

The tension between controlling the cost of labour and the need
to devote resources to training is becoming acute for many retail
firms, especially as the sales environment becomes more difficult.

This tension has led some firms to adopt a very short-term and superficial approach to the problem, which may leave them vulnerable to dangers further ahead. The importance of training is likely to grow, but will vary among sub-sectors of retailing. Richard Weir emphasizes the need to see a positive return on training investment:

The problem is that you have to get the benefit of these improvements in your business in the most tangible form, for example the bottom line of profit and loss account. Retailing in the United Kingdom is uniquely competitive. The phenomenon of multiple competitiveness doesn't give retailers much opportunity to make mistakes in terms of policies that don't pay off. If you try and invest more in your staff, it has got to have a pay-off. If it doesn't your business goes under. If your competitors can provide a service for their customers which involves low expenditure areas like staff, then they are going to beat you. Even though they may not be quite as attractive in terms of the sort of staff which they have, if they in total provide a better or cheaper service then they are going to beat you.

Training is, however, taking on a more important and, for retailing, novel role in the context of recruitment. One way to meet the problem of diminished labour supply is to use the idea of stable and long-term employment as a recruitment device. Within this package, training is of the essence. An emerging strategy is therefore to raise the profile of training so as to facilitate mobility within the organization. As Garfield Davies views it, training can become a major tool of personnel policy which helps to motivate and bind staff to the organization: 'Training itself can be such a big motivater. Almost at times it doesn't matter what you are training, because pulling somebody away from their normal daily job and putting them on a training programme is a very good motivator. Suddenly they are important and the business is taking a specific interest in them.' As will be seen, the clearer and more structured role of training in the John Lewis Partnership is a potential advantage in recruitment.

Training and recruitment have become more closely interlinked, since it is essential to minimize turnover among employees who are given expensive training. One approach—culled from the United States, admits John Hardman—is therefore to pay greater attention to the recruitment of the right people in the first place: 'In terms of training, we focus on recruitment techniques. We aim to get the "people-oriented employees in the first place". We looked at the United States where they do this, recruit people who are good at service. Then they keep them through use of benefits.' Richard Weir, however, believes that the retailing sector has little reason to be proud of its training record: 'In fact the way things are going, more and more companies are suffering from a lack of training. It is somewhat frightening the way we seem to be training people to a much lesser extent than our international competitors.'

No hard evidence exists on the role of recruitment in John Lewis, but there is a strong impression that applicants are evaluated partly on the basis of their likely identification with the Partnership's goals and style of work. Interviews with middle-level staff suggest that an unusually high proportion of them have relatives who also work for the Partnership; the family connection would help to socialize and inform potential employees. Once in the Partnership, managers especially are encouraged to appreciate the peculiar nature of the company. A recruit who does not seem to identify with the Partnership would be assisted to move on, on a friendly basis, rather than be at odds with the prevailing ethos.

Motivation, Remuneration, and Communication

Training of staff is a necessary but insufficient condition for providing the best all around service to the retail customer. Given the potency of first impressions and the difficulty of monitoring, staff must be properly motivated in their work. The potential customers' impression of a retailer may be very unstable or volatile, based heavily on a particular interaction with staff; quite trivial details and circumstances may make a difference. Thus the staff's behaviour is more important than in business interactions that take place over a longer period of time. Yet managers clearly cannot observe the actual performance of all staff at all times. consequently, the firm must attempt to provide incentives (both financial and non-financial) that will encourage appropriate behaviour even when the worker is not observed.

On the financial side, firms have introduced a range of mechanisms that augment the employee's normal pay. These vary from the traditional commission to profit-share and equity-based schemes, and may operate at the department, shop, or firm level. Although some retailers still use commissions, many others have come to believe that they provide the wrong incentives, encouraging overzealous attention to the customer and pressured selling, which hurts the business's reputation in the long term. The more modern schemes are intended to strengthen the commitment of staff to the goals of the firm. Seldom is the success of such schemes tested, except at the informal level of a senior manager asking a number of staff what they think. In some areas, there is considerable scepticism. Profit-sharing, says Garfield Davies, 'is only another form of payment. Once a person receives a profit-share it ceases to stir any kind of job satisfaction'.

Roger Saoul is similarly unimpressed with the concept of profit-related pay: 'We are not traditionally interested in the idea of profit-related pay or similar things. We reward merit. We do have a salary-related bonus. Profit-sharing takes place through distribution of shares. There are share options at the senior level. We offer cheap meals. There is a non-contributory pension. We offer welfare measures, including after retirement.' Others, like Sir Iain Maclaurin, are more positive: 'We have a company level profit-share scheme which provides an incentive for people to get more involved. At present it affects over half the workforce.' The more widespread such schemes become, the less their potential benefit to the retailer. The extra reward becomes normal rather than exceptional. The key issue, Sir Terence Conran recognizes, is whether the incentive remains:

I suppose the question mark always is how real is the incentive effect, because as the organization gets larger people's ability to feel that they have really influenced things gets diluted. Now share options at the top three or four levels of management are just part of a standard package and don't really command the unique interest which one originally hoped for. It becomes part of the package and you have to have it.

In this area, the John Lewis Partnership is clearly a pioneer, and remains well ahead of the competition. The bonus has been paid in most years since 1924 and, as Table 12.1 shows, is a much higher proportion of pay than in any other retailing firm. Of course, the reasons for the Partnership bonus pre-date any recent instrumental theory of motivation, but the benefits are none the less available. Over the last ten years, all of the Partnership's main competitors have introduced profit-sharing schemes of one sort or another.

Non-financial mechanisms focus on communication and the strengthening of the so-called corporate culture. Some companies promulgate a statement of the firm's objectives, typically including some form of commitment to good service for its own sake, and increasingly likely to make reference to the environment. Others pursue a more general strategy of improving the flow of communications within the firm. The emphasis tends to be on top-down information, but most companies make at least some extra provision for reverse communication flows. A typical view is Richard Weir's, that inolvement is the key to success: 'I am a very firm believer that retailing needs a high level of staff involvement. If you start getting people involved in the company they work harder, for they are working for *our* company rather than the company, because they are a shareholder. This works exceedingly well in smallish companies, but is much more difficult in larger companies.'

An appropriate combination of the financial and non-financial may be the best approach. At ASDA, John Hardman seeks to use the Japanese *team leader* example, but utilizes profit incentives as well. Sir Terence Conran outlines the Storehouse approach:

There is no doubt that carefully constructed incentives in a large operation like ours can work, but it is a big question as to how you manage them and make them work. We have a group-wide credit card which works well in the small shops because of the face-to-face of staff to customer. In a larger space it is difficult to persuade staff to use the thing. But turn on a small financial incentive in a properly structured way and the thing turns round instantly.

In all cases there is a paradox: successful customer service cannot be generated entirely by instrumental means—there must be at least some real *warmth*. To take an example from air travel, customer service is marketed with images of happy, caring personnel: to borrow a phrase from Hochschild (1983), airline stewardesses must *really mean* their smiles. The management, as S. Smith (1988) sees it, therefore faces a need to commercialize human feeling. This presents a major challenge with its own in-built contradictions, needing a careful approach if it is not to backfire seriously.[3]

This is an intrinsically difficult problem and the research of Flanders *et al.* cautions against any conclusion that John Lewis has achieved a markedly different work orientation among its staff. Measuring customer service is extremely difficult in any case. In its favour, however, the John Lewis Partnership has a long tradition of both financial and non-financial benefits and incentives, together with a business principle that customer service is at the heart of success. As we have seen, the experience of Spedan Lewis in revitalizing a derelict shop bought in the 1930s suggests a basically successful approach.

Corporate Culture and Communication as Management Tools

Partly as a response to pressures on the human resource side of the business, many retailing firms now claim to take seriously the issue of a deliberately fostered corporate culture. Typically, this means increasing communication, almost entirely in a top-down direction. It may also involve some sort of articulation of corporate

---

[3] At the 1989 USDAW conference a number of delegates expressed anger and dismay at the extra responsibility and pressure placed on them in new customer-care schemes introduced by large retailing firms. Tesco was the company most frequently named.

objectives, which often includes a stated commitment to customer service and a concern with staff welfare. The method is normally intended to work by diffusing ideas and ideals from the top managers downwards. As John Hardman explains: '[The company] does aim for a corporate culture. We train managers in this first. In the late 1970s, we carried out a poll which indicated that the staff thought very little of the managers. We reckoned that if we can inculcate values in managers then they'll spread these to the rest of the staff.'

In some firms, the idea of a corporate culture that emphasizes the commitment of the staff is a longer-established concept. Lower turnover is effectively a prerequisite for the fostering of any durable corporate culture. At Marks and Spencer, says Roger Saoul: 'Our corporate culture is very different [from other firms] and very important. About one-quarter of the staff have more than ten years service. There is a long-term commitment which leads to a two-way exchange.'

One chairman noted that the major upheavals in the industry had led to certain forced patterns of behaviour and attitude, under considerable competitive pressure. Consequently, in Sir Iain Maclaurin's opinion, Tesco's corporate culture emerged by default: it simply arose from 'saving the company from going to the dogs'.

Retailers now put considerable emphasis on in-house communication, reacting to a past in which the attitudes and orientations of the staff were regarded as largely irrelevant. Most companies use a range of media to relay information to the staff throughout the company and believe such communication helps diffuse a particular corporate culture. David Sainsbury observes:

We started within our accounts department with a set of corporate objectives which are spelt out. We then try to communicate these to everyone. So, in terms of company results people know how well we are doing. At the year end, we have a corporate video and an employee report which goes to staff. Directors talk to all the area managers and deputy managers and then they go back to their stores and talk to the other levels within the store. So you do get a very substantial amount of communication.

The John Lewis Partnership has been well ahead of the field in its efforts to communicate with employees. The extensive range of in-house journalism, at both store and company levels, dates back to before the Second World War. Other retailers offer nothing resembling the Partnership employees' right to direct anonymous letters to management and expect a reply. And partners have been receiving financial information about the business since 1929, when the new Partnership company issued its first set of accounts. In sum, the recent efforts of other retailers to improve communication and a sense of corporate culture look quite primitive from the Partnership's point of view.

The executives interviewed for this study seldom mentioned the main union in the industry, the USDAW, but showed no apparent hostility or belief that the union represented any sort of impediment to the objectives of management. If anything, John Hardman's comments suggest quite the reverse: 'Communication is done through store councils where all staff members are represented. We have very good relations with USDAW although they were a bit slow with their support at first. Now their shop stewards are trained by us.'

The emphasis, time and again, is on telling the staff about the firm and what the management are doing, with videos used as a normal working tool. At Tesco, says Sir Iain Maclaurin, 'The chairman chairs the Communication Committee. We use video a lot, on a weekly basis. There are managers' associations.' Some retailers have attempted a more two-way approach. Storehouse attempts to engage the staff in discussion about the pattern of work rewards and the organization of the work itself. Sir Terence Conran is quite enthusiastic in his support for these initiatives and believes they will pay off:

For example at the moment ... in one of our chains we provide staff services of various kinds. We are going through store by store, literally asking the question which would you prefer to have. Do we go on providing these expensive staff restaurants or would you prefer the freedom to decide and have X added to your pay packet? Another example is our annual conference when all store managers are assembled in one place with the merchandise. They are asked about product ranges and practices. All conference delegates have a keyboard in front of them to allow them to answer. It's on the form of carefully programmed section questions. There is no doubt that the importance of this is increasingly recognized.

Seldom is any explicit attempt made to gauge the impact of the communication mechanisms. Most managers have little idea of the effectiveness of in-house communications. David Sainsbury saw no need for formal measurements and voiced a typically sanguine belief in the efficacy of store visits and general contact with staff:

We tried doing some attitude surveys, it just tended to be too broad and too long and was not really useful. I think we find other ways of communicating with staff, visiting the stores and so on. I think that probably gives you better and quicker information on individual stores. There are these two different issues. One is, do people feel that a particular pay structure is fair across the company and you get a very quick feedback. The second question is, is x or y not a happy branch because it's got a manager who's not coping.

Some companies emerge as rather more sensitive than others to the problem of integrating the workforce into a single corporate entity. John Hardman suggest regional variations may make a single national strategy inappropriate: 'You find that in some parts of the country, there is a loyalty to the store, rather than the company. This is not so in the south and south-east, but its true in many other areas, especially the north and Scotland.'

Approaches vary considerably, perhaps because the whole concept of corporate culture and employee relations is so new. Whilst some firms are very keen to stress a consistent pattern and homogeneity across the often considerable extent of the workforce, others try a different line. Roger Saoul, for example, sees the Marks and Spencer care and concern as based very much on the individual.

It is not widely recognized that badly designed and implemented schemes to encourage a particular corporate culture have the potential to do some damage. Garfield Davies, however, identified an inherent tension in the process of integrating the employee to the organization, if the organization's underlying goal is to make a profit, as it almost certainly is. It is difficult to motivate people through essentially instrumental means to invest *emotional capital* in their work tasks:

I think the mistake is, they have got the customer in mind. You keep instilling in an employee, 'you are working for the customer, we want their money, and it's your job to do the right thing to get their money'. I think it is much better to say, 'you are the person we are concerned with, you are working for us. We want you to know about the business, you are part of the business. You believe in the business, the business believes in you.' This will reflect itself automatically in the employee–customer relationship. It is developing the employees' awareness without actually telling them that it is the customer who pays the money. If you get the employees more identified, then they will automatically relate to the customers in the way that the employer is suggesting he wants.

The problem of communication remains a vexed one for any organization. The John Lewis Partnership has gone further than any other retailer, and for many more years. Even so, Flanders *et al.* find that grievances remain among Partnership employees, and the main result of the extensive communication may be to legitimate management. On the positive side, it is also likely that the Partnership would become aware more quickly than other firms if any innovation in work or training practices led to discontent among employees or conflicts in expectations. This feedback is likely to become more important as the pace of change accelerates.

Problems from the Worker's Perspective

Competitive pressures have forced retailers to accord a more important role to human resources. Some of the changes in retailing, however, have generated their own tensions, which tend to undermine the role of individual workers and threaten their working conditions. These tendencies arise out of the growing use of technology, the development of superstores, and the greater flexibility demanded of labour. The costs of these developments may not always be fully appreciated by managers as they design changes in their human resource programmes.

From a labour process perspective, the increased use of electronic point-of-sale and related technology in warehousing and distribution could be seen as part of an attempt to reduce individual autonomy and promote deskilling—plausible employer tactics at a time of incipient labour shortage. The use of electronic point-of-sale terminals has typically been explained in terms of their ability to gather information about the sales of the store; however, the technology is equally capable to generating data about the employee. At J. Sainsbury and elsewhere, worker productivity on check-out terminals is now liable to be measured, very accurately, and the information used for setting performance targets. Such practices may seem to devalue the quality of the job, making it still more difficult to secure the *emotional commitment* characteristic of a helpful and cheerful staff. In other respects too, an emphasis on crude productivity may damage the quality of service. For example, the move to remote, out-of-town shopping centres can make recruitment difficult, since there are costs for staff having to travel at variable and unsocial hours. This too can undermine the service goal.

Many managers do not recognize the disadvantages of the flexibiliy in working hours which may be crucial in retailing. It is true that certain categories of workers, such as married women with children who are free only in the afternoon, appreciate the ability to have working hours tailored for their needs. Said David Sainsbury: 'There is no conflict with the need for flexibility of staff. We can fit in around the needs of employees. For example there are some people who only want to work on Sundays.' To many other staff, however, such flexibility is disruptive—a problem too often overlooked, in the view of Garfield Davies.

While the John Lewis Partnership is not immune to these dangers, it is less likely than other firms to ignore worker feedback. The long-established emphasis on the human side of the business highlights issues that might not be raised effectively in a conventional firm. As people become scarcer and the value of training capitalized in employees grows, the need not to annoy or alienate the workforce will be crucial. Partnership principles are designed to obviate this possibility, and the historical experience of the Partnership suggests a large measure of success.

A Strategic Approach to Human Resources

Although new pressures are forcing a new consideration of the use of people in retailing, the sector has not yet developed a detailed strategy for human resources which would stand comparison with strategic thinking on, say, financial resources or investment. The interconnected nature of the problems discussed above is encouraging more systematic thinking, however. Some observers have conceived of a new sort of workforce, in which the inevitable flexibility of work assignments is embedded in a stable, salaried career structure, backed by regular training and retraining. Such an approach could ameliorate the recruitment problem and, by reducing turnover, should make it easier to gain employees' long-term commitment to the firm's objectives.

It is important to recognize that such hopes for the future represent a near-revolutionary change in the role of labour in the sector, and hence may be unrealistic. The tension between short-term costs and long-term gain, so characteristic of much of British industry, is likely to be exacerbated by upward pressure on wage costs over the medium-term future. Yet the combination of labour supply pressures and competition in the product market will continue to push retailing firms in this new direction.

The new strategic thinking has appeared in response to problems that clearly cannot be solved by traditional methods. To take an example, the role of the manager, as John Hardman sees it, is gradually being redefined into that of customer liaison: 'We are trying to systematize our store management as much as possible to release managers for the task of dealing with customers, and to release labour generally.' More generally, Sir Terence Conran recognizes that the reduced availability of labour is pushing firms towards a quite different conception of the workforce: 'Employee availability is a problem: we want a more full-time and dedicated workforce. We're emphasizing career development and better pay.' John Hardman likewise supports this ideal of a less casual, more professional workforce: 'The aim is for a professional, pensionable, salaried workforce, and getting away from casual labour.'

The limits to the use of technology are now beginning to be established, with many chairmen returning to basics in the search for a more committed workforce. As David Sainsbury's comments show, this means analysing the identification of workers with the goals of the firm and looking at the content of the job itself:

Bringing in computers does not make the work less interesting. Ten years ago, if you asked how much of a product was sold last week, the manager wouldn't know. Now he does. In that sense we have got much better information. And it does take away some of the dreary jobs. More fundamental issues are about whether employees agree with the goals of the organization. Do they think they are giving a service to the community and the customer? Are employees proud of the company's performance? I think these are more fundamental questions than just pure technology.

Garfield Davies believes that the training and employment of people should service multiple purposes: '[Increasing flexibility of tasks] would make a much better employee. Specialization at certain levels is important I suppose. But to have someone performing a mundane operation, however essential it is, I don't think enhances their job satisfaction and it doesn't contribute to the well-being of the operation.

Few firms have yet progressed far beyond identifying the general nature of the problem. The solutions adopted so far have generally been *ad hoc* and tentative; many of these attempts seem destined to fail and sometimes even to make things worse. Anita Roddick observes:

Customer care is often translated as selling a product, it's going up to a customer, finding out his needs, and selling him the product and getting him out of the shop as fast as you can. Customer care with us is entirely different . . . it's an environment which is pleasant, it's an environment that is engaging, smells great, you can put the products on your body without paying for them, and you can chat to the staff.

It is striking that when major retailers talk about the role of people in their organizations, they come very close to repeating what Spedan Lewis, founder of the John Lewis Partnership, observed at the beginning of the century. As we have seen, Spedan Lewis identified the weaknesses of his father's approach to the business in his attitude to the staff. In many respects a successful retailer, John Lewis senior was held back by his neglect of the human dimension. The Partnership's competitors in the early 1990s are coming to a similar conclusion: putting the staff first is not only sensible, it is also increasingly a *sine qua non* for business success.

Conclusion

Changes in the demand and supply for labour have fundamentally altered the importance of the human side of retailing, which is now widely recognized as central to the competitive process. Retailers need flexible, reliable, and able staff at the shop-floor level, trained and motivated to give good service to the customer; they also require high-quality decision-makers, recruited from a wider background than in the past. And this human capability must be harnessed through a system of good pay, effective communication, and a strategic emphasis on the needs and aspirations of the personnel of the organization.

For many firms this new pattern is still more theory than practice; others have introduced a wide range of innovations and put much greater public emphasis on the human side (for example in their annual reports), but their ultimate success is not yet clear. Indeed, many chairmen realize that the new model of human relations will take time to achieve. Nevertheless, the general direction of change is clear.

As we have seen, the John Lewis Partnership is ahead of its competitors in virtually every aspect of human resource strategy.

In fact, the Partnership Principles could be described as a blueprint for such a strategy. Such a view misses the ethical dimension of Spedan Lewis's thought, but it does capture some of the essential thinking of businesses that underlies the John Lewis approach. Other retailing firms are now trying to emulate key aspects of those Principles, but without fundamentally altering their ownership and control structures. Just how successful they will be in the longer term remains to be seen.

13

Conclusion

A major theme of this study has been that corporate performance cannot be adequately understood solely in terms of the conventional framework based on neo-classical economics and its derivatives, such as the theory of finance. This chapter takes a closer look at the conventional framework and its limitations.

Economics has long been methodologically separated from the other social sciences, a disjunction that has had considerable influence on the orthodox views of business practitioners. Because of the domination of neo-classical economics and its methodological precepts, a very restricted and rigid view of human agency and motivation has prevailed. Thinking in terms of rational actors significantly limits one's ability to explain human behaviour. The range of human interaction and experience in the sociology of organizations is largely ignored in the economics literature, or treated as a minor issue.

A second problem is the failure of management accounting to broaden its scope over the last fifty years. The framework of accounting is derived primarily from the needs of business in the first half of this century. As a result, it is not well suited to the needs of the current day, which are quite different. In particular, the traditional accounting framework does not pay enough attention to the human side of business. Indeed it considers labour only as a cost, rather than seeing human resources as an asset.

The Split between Economics and Other Social Sciences

Within the social sciences, economics (and to a degree political science) is divided from the other disciplines by a deep rift.

C. Taylor (1985) speaks of a 'global war between the heirs of the Enlightenment and the Romantics', which manifests itself in 'the struggle between technology and the sense of history or community'. The viewpoint of economics is associated with 'instrumental reason versus the intrinsic values of certain forms of life' and with 'the domination of nature versus the need for reconciliation with nature' (Taylor 1985: p. 246).

The methodological debates that pervade social theory have left their mark on organization theory in particular. Managerial writers, who see themselves as contributing to a practical and largely value-free science, pursue prescriptive, technocratic aims, while other authors, with more social-scientific aspirations, focus on analysing an important area of contemporary society. The latter group comprises both broadly structural-functionalist inclinations and more subjective, interpretive approaches. Within the interpretive tradition, some writers adhere to a politically radical perspective. The full complexity of the field is best understood at the level of methodology.

The strength of orthodox economics, and the conventional wisdom derived from it, is that the profession has developed a relatively robust set of agreed methodological principles. At the core is an axiomatic and individualist theory of rational action. (As discussed further below, this means essentially that decision-makers are presumed to make consistent choices among available options.) These principles are so powerful and flexible that they have dominated all mainstream economic work and have spilled over into related areas such as political science and even biology. But it has proved difficult to integrate economic thinking with that of any other area of the social sciences.

Organization Theory: Methodological Strands

From the beginning of the century some organizational writers and practitioners have been concerned purely with increasing business (and usually industrial) efficiency. This goal is certainly not incompatible with a careful and honest appraisal of the subject, but neither does it require the wider perspective and more self-consciously methodical analysis of academic social scientists. Certain classic works on organizations have tried to satisfy both the needs of practitioners and the methodological standards of social science, but since the 1950s, as the field grew and developed self-confidence, less effort has been made to reconcile these two strands in the literature.

During the last twenty years there has been a revolt against positivistic methods in sociology. This new departure has several sources:

1. A recognition that it is important to understand the point of view of the agents being observed and analysed; their actions take place in a subjective frame of reference that is only indirectly related to the world as perceived by the objective researcher.
2. The realization that power and conflict lie at the very heart of social behaviour, in the sense that interests at every level are only partially reconcilable.
3. A rejection of functional thinking as a dominant mode of explanation.

Giddens (1987) gives an overview of these themes in the context of the social sciences as a whole; Reed (1985) discussed organization theory specifically. These criticisms, whilst directed primarily to mainstream economics and positivist sociology, apply to a great deal of organizational writing also.

Any successful social theoretical framework will have to embrace both:

1. individuals acting in a conscious, purposive manner in pursuit of goals that are chosen independently of their environment; and
2. individuals living in society—a process that both subtly alters that society and contributes to its reproduction. By acquiring and using the social knowledge needed to be a citizen, individuals maintain features of the system.

Economics: The Philosophy of Rational Action

Modern neo-classical economics might best be characterized as the study of rational behaviour in a subset of human social activity. Rationality is therefore intrinsic to the ways in which economists have investigated these social phenomena. This emphasis can be traced to the Anglo-Saxon philosophical tradition of empiricism and a rejection of Hegelian idealistic speculation. Econometrics is central to the profession; in contrast, the statistical sides of other social sciences are far less dominant. As a result, economists have been bound by a rather restricted sense of what constitutes acceptable data and evidence.

The economist's emphasis on rationality has encountered a number of objections. For example, critics have argued that:

1. The model of rationality used is not very rich or powerful, and so cannot really get at the truth of human action.
2. People are seldom rational; they are apt to be misled by themselves and by others, and to behave in ways that cannot be interpreted within the theory of rational choice.
3. The emphasis on rationality is itself an ideological contribution to the status quo, so that economics merely justifies rather than explains.
4. The emphasis on rationality inevitably slights the moral dimension of the social sciences; economics seeks to reduce all *ought* questions to ones of *is*.

Whilst it is impossible to do justice to these issues here, a few general points are in order. First, on the question of ethical considerations, neo-classical economics goes to great lengths to qualify its prescriptive statements. The central notion of distributive justice in welfare economics is the Pareto criterion. A situation is Pareto-optimal (or Pareto-efficient) if any change would make some party worse off. As a test of real-world policies, the Pareto standard has very little practical relevance. Its importance in economics owes far less to its ethical basis than to its operational efficacy (that is, it works well in mathemetical models).

The charge that economists' emphasis on rationality helps to perpetuate the status quo touches on an enduring theme in classical sociology. The idea that there is something inherently unattractive about rationality as such is an important argument for understanding the problems of industrial society, whether in a Marxian or in a Weberian/Durkheimian framework. The historical antipathy to political economists from at least as far back as Burke ties in closely with a feeling that rational analysis is itself disenchanting and unwelcome. The sociological basis for this feeling is the myth of a pre-industrial golden age, when relations between persons were not poisoned with rational considerations. At the micro level, it is well known that individual motivation goes beyond pure instrumental calculation, as many organization theorists recognize (Argyris 1964). Economics has grave difficulty embracing such ideas.

The first two criticisms cited above address the fundamentals of economic theory. The basis of neo-classical economics is an axiomatic model of rational behaviour. In this model agents are considered to be rational in the sense that they make consistent choices between available options. In other words, if an individual prefers *a* to *b*, and *b* to *c*, he will never prefer *c* to *a*. But this is a model of procedural rationality only. It does not rule out anti-social actions (collectively irrational actions), or suicide, or behaviour that just seems plain bizarre to the rest of us. By the economist's standard, people who believe in witchcraft, astrology, and the flatness of the earth are not necessarily irrational. Following Elster (1983c), this is a thin theory of rationality. The textbook model of economic man requires supplementary assumptions about greed (non-satiation of wants) and material aspirations.

Neo-classical economists are not troubled by the lack of a more substantive theory. By considering optimal behaviour, Binmore and Dasgupta (1986) observe, economists can short-circuit the vastly more problematic question of how people actually behave. Elster (1979) argues persuasively that a generalized capacity for seeking global, as opposed to local, optima is a diagnostic feature of human agency. Admittedly this need not imply that such a capacity is used in all areas of life.

The rational action model implies an individualistic methodology that distinguishes economics from most work in sociology and organizational behaviour. The economist's approach may avoid the dangers of functionalist thinking, but not those of reductionism: concepts such as class, company, and work-group can only be understood in so far as they can be reduced to aggregations of individuals. A second difficulty is that the rational action approach takes the preferences of individuals as given, ignoring the whole question of how tastes, prejudices, and attitudes are formed. Whilst economists recognize that preferences may change over time, they see little possibility of modelling these processes successfully. The primacy of formal modelling in economics makes it impossible for economics to incorporate most empirical work done in social psychology and sociology—even though this work flatly contradicts many of the core propositions of orthodox economics.

With all its limitations, the neo-classical approach would never have endured if it did not also have important strengths. It can explain a great deal about the economic phenomena of production, distribution, and exchange. The deficiencies of the model are likely to be less serious in those areas of life where calculative, instrumental, rational decision-making pays off. Thus, for example, the economist would expect the conventional framework to provide a useful way of conceptualizing the issues related to financial markets, but not to explain all aspects of their operation. Similarly, when acting as consumers or producers, most people appear to know what they want and how to get it. If we allow that preferences are socially created and that people care about matters such as freedom, self-respect, and other citizen virtues, then the room for economics to contribute to these questions is correspondingly reduced, as the best practitioners have recognized.

Despite the historical gap between economics and the other social sciences, a more unified approach to explaining human economic behaviour may eventually prove possible. Social theory has moved in the direction of methodological individualism, while modern economic theory has attempted much more intricate explorations of rational behaviour. The problem in any integrative theory will be to find a balance between the rational and non-rational elements of human behaviour.

Accounting Perspectives: Performance at the Operational Level

Since the function of accounting, within a company, is to provide information for managerial decision-making, one would expect competitive pressures to have encouraged the evolution of effective accounting systems. Yet it has been charged that the accountant's perspective often hinders the effective definition, measurement, and control of business performance. One problem, it is argued, is that financial accounting dominates the assessment of performance. Another is that the failure to update the framework of management accounting has led to distorted decision-making. In particular, the human contribution to performance has been severely understated.

The first charge is perhaps most often made in the United Kingdom, reflecting a more general discontent with the balance of influence and power between financial and industrial capital. Over a number of decades, the argument runs, a strong financial sector has developed independent of manufacturing; as a result, the services of the one are not well matched with the needs of the other. City–industry relations have been marked by a lack of long-term commitment and a consequent paucity of funding for the longer-term industrial investment. Government policy has tended to favour meeting the apparent needs of the City, sometimes at the expense of industry.

This controversial argument (not to be developed further here) has some implications for our assessment of the John Lewis Partnership. To the extent that a financial bias induces a short-term perspective, the Partnership's relative distance from the capital markets may have had positive consequences. Moreoever, protection from external capital markets accords with the thinking of Spedan Lewis on the role of finance.

The second strand of criticism focuses on the managerial accounting function, which captures information on costs and profitability that relates directly to the production process. Managers use this information in making decisions about the enterprise in both the short and the long term. Several critiques (Hayes and Abernathy 1980; Kaplan 1984; Johnson and Kaplan 1987) charge that the information provided simply does not jibe with the realities of modern corporate performance. Consequently, actual managerial cost accounting systems 'provided few benefits to organisations' (Johnson and Kaplan 1987: 12).

Specific failings of conventional management accounting systems include:

1. Inappropriate allocation of overheads; too often these are allocated on the basis of direct labour costs, even when such costs constitute a very small proportion of the total. Such allocations can give seriously misleading indications of the relative profitability of different products.

2. Inappropriate time horizons; the quarterly and monthly periods of accounting reports are both too long and too short. On the one hand, managers need very short-term information in order to adjust production quickly; they would like to have data that are less complete but more timely than accounting figures. On the other hand, many decisions, especially those related to research and development, human resources, and investments in quality, should be evaluated over a much longer time period. The bias towards quarterly and even annual accounts, with short-term profit as the main objective, distorts decisions in these areas.

3. The problem of evaluating intangible assets, such as brands, customer loyalty, supplier goodwill, research and development expertise and applications, and the human resources of the firm. Balance sheets that fail to reflect these items may give a radically distorted impression of the affairs of the firm. Of course it is difficult to place a value on such intangibles, but it seems clear that a wider range of information is needed if, for example, the stock market is to do its job properly.

Recent developments in global competition have heightened the importance of these deficiencies in accounting systems. For example total quality-control programmes, which aim for zero defects, are difficult to reconcile with the conventional accounting procedures. Quality strategies pay off primarily at the selling and marketing end of the business, and such links in the chain of competitive advantage are not well identified in the usual accounts.

But perhaps the biggest problem, and the one of most direct interest to the service industries, especially retailing, lies in the evaluation of human resources, which represent an important potential for productivity and competitive advantage. Since human effort and initiative are so elastic, the adoption of a successful new personnel strategy can generate a major improvement in performance, yet it would be difficult to trace this change in the conventional accounts.

What might be done to supplement and improve the measurement of human resources and to place some sort of human capital on the balance sheet? In some instances, the real worth of a company is informally known to be bound up in one or two star employees. In such cases, the market valuation of the firm is likely to drop if the key talent departs. But this principle is applicable more widely and needs to be made as systematic as possible.

Business Ethics: Broader Views of Performance

In the last century large corporations have amassed economic and perhaps political power to rival that of the smaller nation states. In such a world, many have questioned whether the pursuit of self-interest is an appropriate corporate or indeed national goal. Partly in response to this public perception, firms have learned to use ethical arguments as part of the competitive process: cultivating an image of honesty, public service, and national responsibility helps to sell the product.

Some firms have always had a strong sense of superordinate goals, independent of the potential competitive benefit. Often a prior ethical point of view, enshrined in the business practice and culture of the firm, has incidentally turned out to be of commercial value. This pattern is by no means to be equated with manipulative posturing to serve public relations purposes. At the same time, genuine ethical principles on the part of corporate leaders may coexist with a sense that these principles can be turned to useful commercial advantage.

Now more than ever, business ethics is an important issue for firms, and for public discussion, for at least two reasons. First, affluence characteristically generates a demand for the removal of the negative side effects that accompany large-scale production, for example, air and water pollution. This concern may wax and wane, but it appears to have increased over the long term, as reflected in the heightened attention to green issues in the developed world. Second, the potential for voluntarist, private solutions to the problems of society has increased as the ideological and political attack on the role of the state has intensified. In both the United Kingdom and the United States, government proposals to alleviate youth unemployment and inner-city blight have appealed to corporations to act from a sense of civic duty and pride. Business itself has generally embraced the rhetoric of such an approach, although it is not clear how much concrete action has resulted. We have, in a sense, been here before. Many years ago some observers perceived a managerial revolution that involved the development of increased social responsibility (Burnham 1942). Viewing their responsibilities as much wider than simply covering the interests of shareholders, the new managers were concerned with the impact of their decisions on the public at large and attempted to exercise their new power in society responsibly.

The *soulful corporation* turned out to be, if not a myth, then certainly rather an exaggerated concept. Adjustment to economic shocks in the 1970s was not significantly tempered at the firm level by a sense of corporate social responsibility: indeed this option was not available for firms fighting to survive. In response to the government-imposed limits to the supply of money of the early 1980s, corporations in the United Kingdom and the United States cut capacity and behaved just like any textbook profit-maximizer. However, the economic growth and development of the 1980s has been accompanied by considerable interest in the ethical context of business, and its relevance to commercial success. This discussion, like so many others, has often begun with the experience of Japan, where a commitment to national and societal goals seems characteristic of many large and successful corporations.

This commitment has both internal and external consequences that may build competitive advantage. Inside the firm, employees and managers may be more easily and more naturally motivated when there is some unifying theme, particularly when it is not obviously self-serving. As the sociological perspective suggests, people have an essentially moral nature. In some Japanese firms this ethical theme may be reinforced by a socialization process designed to instil both formal and substantive beliefs in the workforce; corporate constitutions, mottos, or songs may all play a part. Externally, a deliberate ethical perspective may help in developing mutually beneficial longer-term relations with customers and suppliers. The gains from high-trust relationships are well known. Deliberate attempts to create trust, however, may be self-defeating (Parfit 1984), if the gain-seeking motivation is transparent.

Paradoxically, then, although an ethical approach to business behaviour may convey certain benefits, such gains are not likely to be achieved when they are deliberately sought. There needs to be a higher order commitment to certain types of behaviour for its own sake. However, corporations can probably benefit from taking the ethical dimension seriously rather than seeing it as a costly and peripheral extra. Most organization members have an ethical basis for their decisions, even if it is not well articulated. Unrecognized in neo-classical economics, the ethical premises of individual decision-making are often hidden or played down, but they are there, and provide a basis to work from. The big obstacle is the belief that such considerations are at best an irrelevance and at worst a direct hindrance to effective business performance.

Conclusion

The conventional wisdom that economic performance is best understood in terms of ownership, control, and the influence of capital markets, is flawed in three main ways. First, it is based on a clearly defined but very limited view of human actions and motivation taken from neo-classical economics. The wider perspective on the human dimension found in the other social sciences is largely absent, partly because these other disciplines have not produced a unified body of theory which can challenge economist head on and meet the (possibly spurious) standards of rigour and mathematical tractability. Second, the tools of operational performance measurement are outdated, not only in their emphasis on the financial side but also in their failure to take seriously a number of intangible elements in the firm's performance. Chief among these is the human capital input to the enterprise.

Closely related to both of these problems is a third obstacle: the neglect of the ethical side of business. Any organization that involves human beings inevitably contains a moral dimension. Modern work on rational action is uncovering the links between ethical principles and achievement of self-interested goals (M. Taylor 1987). To act on these links is difficult, but evidence from Japan suggests it is not impossible. The John Lewis Partnership is founded on precisely such a combination of ethical principle and business insight.

Further Research

Any case study suffers from the limitations of specificity, just as it gains from the richness of detail. The success of the John Lewis Partnership offers a convincing counter-argument to the predictions of the conventional economics literature. Indeed it suggests that this literature is severely flawed.

A new framework for the analysis of business performance is clearly needed, one which preserves what is robust from the financial and economic literature, but which embodies a much richer conception of what constitutes business success. We have outlined such a framework in this chapter. Further work is needed both to develop a metholology and to collect empirical data.

Data collection will be the key to more detailed analysis of the true determinants of performance. This study of the John Lewis Partnership suggests that a particularly important task will be to explore the role of service and the customer/assistant interface. A second important issue is the role of career development and the allocation of human resources over time within the firm. How can firms use these resources strategically? On such questions, the concerns of academics and practitioners overlap (see e.g. Caruso 1990). By constructively exploiting this convergence of interest, we can assemble a body of richer and deeper data that will greatly enhance our understanding of business performance. This task is central to the London School of Economics Business Performance Group.

The John Lewis Partnership in Context

The John Lewis Partnership is unusual in being employee-owned, but also in having benefited from the extraordinary influence and imagination of its founder, John Spedan Lewis. The Partnership's sixty-year history has been marked by great continuity in structure and practice, a testimony to Lewis's vision. More to the point, one might ask, has it all been a success? From a commercial point of view, the answer is an unqualified yes. After a lacklustre decade immediately following the Second World War, the Partnership built up a formidable reputation in the 1960s and 1970s, which carried it to major success in the 1980s.

Judged by its influence on the world around it, Spedan Lewis's experiment has perhaps been less successful. Several companies have emulated the Partnership or learnt from it, but British business as a whole remains largely ignorant of the principles that underpin the Partnership's commercial success. The founder may have hoped for more in this respect. In the future, however, it seems likely that the Partnership's influence will increase. The most forward-looking retailers are gradually converging on many features of Partnership Principles. The pressures forcing this change—competition, demographics, demand for service, and a new focus on the customer—are increasingly influencing other areas of business as well. The example set by the John Lewis Partnership, especially its view of the human side of business, will be of growing importance in the years to come.

References

ABELL, P. (1985), 'Industrial Democracy, Has it a Future? The West European Experience', *Journal of General Management*, 10: 50–62.

About the John Lewis Partnership (n.d.), John Lewis Partnership.

ABRAMS, M. (1955), 'Developments in the Retail Trade', *The Times Review of Industry*, May.

AKERLOF, G., and YELLEN, J. (1986), *Efficiency Wage Models of the Labour Market* (Cambridge).

ALCHIAN, A., and DEMSETZ, H. (1972), 'Production, Information Costs and Economic Organisation', *American Economic Review*, 62(3) June: 777–95.

AOKI, M. (1984) (ed.), *The Economic Analysis of the Japanese Firm* (Amsterdam).

—— (1988), *Information, Incentives and Bargaining in the Japanese Economy* (Cambridge).

ARGYRIS, C. (1964), *Integrating the Individual and the Organisation* (New York).

ASCH, S., (1956), 'Studies in Independence and Conformity: I. A Minority For One Against a Unanimous Majority', *Psychological Monographs*.

AUERBACH, A. (1988) (ed.), *Corporate Takeovers* (Chicago).

BAMFIELD, J. (1988), 'Competition and Change in British Retailing', *National Westminster Bank Review*, Feb., 15–29.

BARNETT, C. (1984), *The Audit of War* (London).

BATEMAN, B. W. (1987), 'Keynes' Changing Conception of Probability', *Economics and Philosophy*, 3, (1), Apr.

BELL, W., and HANSON, C. (1989), *Profit-Sharing and Profitability* (London).

BERLE, A., and MEANS, G. (1932), *The Modern Corporation and Private Property* (New York).

BINMORE, K. AND DASGUPTA, P. (1986) (eds.), *Economic Organisations as Games* (Oxford).

BLANCHFLOWER, D. G., and OSWALD, A. J. (1987), 'Profit Sharing: Can it Work?', *Oxford Economic Papers*, 39: 1–19.

BRADLEY, K. and ESTRIN, S. (1987), 'Profit Sharing in the Retail Sector: the Relative Performance in the John Lewis Partnership', London School of Economics Centre for Labour Economics Discussion Paper No. 279.

——, ESTRIN, S. and TAYLOR, S. (1990) 'Employee Ownership and Company Performance in the John Lewis Partnership', London School of Economics Business Performance Group, forthcoming, *Industrial Relations*.

——, and GELB, A. (1982) 'The Mondragon Cooperatives: Guidelines for a Cooperative Economy?' in Jones, D. and Svejnar, J. *Participatory and Self-Managed Firms: Evaluating Economic Performance* (Lexington, Mass.)

—— (1983), *Worker Capitalism: the New Industrial Relations* (London).

——, and NEJAD, A. (1989), *Managing Owners* (Cambridge).

BREALY, R., and MYERS, S. (1988), *Principles of Corporate Finance* (London).

Brown, W. (1989), 'Pay Systems', in K. Sisson (ed.) *Personnel Management* (Oxford).

BURNHAM, J. (1942), *The Managerial Revolution* (London).

BURRELL, G., and MORGAN, G. (1979), *Sociological Paradigms and Organisational Analysis* (London).

CARUSO, R. (1990), 'An Examination of Organizational Mentoring: The Case of Motorola', Ph.D. thesis, London University.

CHANNON, D. F. (1978), *The Service Industries: Strategy, Structure and Financial Performance* (Manchester).

CLEGG, H. (1960), *A New Approach to Industrial Democracy* (Oxford).

CONTE, M., and TANNENBAUM, A. (1978), 'Employee Owned Companies: Is the Difference Measurable', *Monthly Labour Review*, 101, (7), July: 23–8.

COSH, A. D. and HUGHES, A. (1988), 'The Anatomy of Corporate Control', *Cambridge Journal of Economics*, 11, (4): 285–313.

DEFOURNEY, J., ESTRIN, S., and JONES, D. C. (1985), 'The Effects of Workers' Participation on Enterprise Performance: Empirical Evidence From French Cooperatives', *International Journal of Industrial Organisation*, 3: 195–217.

DEMESTZ, H. (1988), *Ownership, Control and the Firm* (Oxford).

DODD, T. (1972), *Employee Participation in the John Lewis Partnership*, London School of Economics, Dept. of Industrial Relations.

DORE, R. (1973), *British Factory, Japanese Factory* (London).

—— (1986), *Flexible Rigidities* (London).

—— (1987), *Taking Japan Seriously* (London).

DRUCKER, P. (1989), *The New Realities* (Oxford).

ELSTER, J. (1979), *Ulysses and the Sirens* (Cambridge).

—— (1983*a*), *Explaining Technical Change* (Cambridge).

—— (1983*b*), *Sour Grapes* (Cambridge).

—— (1983*c*) (ed.), *Rational Choice* (Cambridge).

——, and MOENE, K. (1989), (eds.), *Alternatives to Capitalism* (Cambridge).

ESTRIN, S., and WILSON, N. (1986), 'The Microeconomic Effects of Profit-Sharing: The British Experience', London School of Economics Centre for Labour Economics Discussion Paper No. 47, July.

ETZIONI, A. (1961), *A Comparative Analysis of Complex Organisations* (New York).

—— (1969) (ed.), *Readings on Modern Organization*, (Englewood Cliffs, NJ).

EVELY, R. (1959), *Retail Distribution* in Tew, B. and Henderson, R. F. (1959).

FAMA, E., and JENSEN, M. C. (1980), 'Agency Problems and the Theory of the Firm, *Journal of Political Economy*, 88, (2): 288–307.

——, —— (1983), 'Separation of Ownership and Control', *Journal of Law and Economics*, 26, June, 301–25.

FLANDERS, A., POMERANZ, R., and WOODWARD, J. (1968), *Experiment in Industrial Democracy* (London).

FOX, A. (1974), *Beyond Contract* (London).

FUROBOTN, E. (1976), 'The Long Run Analysis of the Labor-Managed Firm: An Alternative Interpretation', *American Economic Review*, 66: 104–24.

GALBRAITH, J. (1967), *The New Industrial State* (London).

GEORGE, K. (1966), *Productivity in Distribution*, Cambridge University Dept. of Applied Economics Occasional Paper No. 8.

GIDDENS, A. (1987), *Social Theory and Modern Sociology* (Cambridge).

GINTIS, H. (1989), 'Financial Markets and the Political Structure of the Enterprise', *Journal of Economic Behaviour and Organisation*, 11: 311–22.

GORMAN, T. (1967), 'Tastes, Habits and Choices', *International Economic Review*, 8: 218–22.

HAYES, R., and ABERNATHY, W. (1980), 'Managing Our Way to Economic Decline', *Harvard Business Review*, July–Aug., 67–77.

HERZBERG, F. (1968), 'One More Time: How Do You Motivate Employees?', *Harvard Business Review*, Jan.–Feb., 53–62.

HILFERDING, R. (1981), *Finance Capital: A Study of the Latest Phase of Capitalist Development* (London).

HOCHSCHILD, A. (1983), *The Managed Heart: The Commercialisation of Human Feeling* (Berkeley, Calif.).

HUMBLE, J. (1989), *Service: the New Competitive Edge* (Brussels).

JEFFREYS, J. B. (1955), 'Shifts in the Distributive Pattern and the Department Store' London Press Exchange Papers No. 2, Nov.

JENSEN, M. C., and MECKLING, W. H. (1979), 'Rights and Production Functions: An Application to Labor-Managed Firms and Codetermination, *Journal of Business*, 52, (4): 469–506.

JOHNSON, G. (1979) (ed.), *Business Strategy and Retailing* (London).

JOHNSON, H., and KAPLAN, R. (1987), *Relevance Lost* (Boston).

JONES, D. C., and SVEJNAR, J. (1985), 'Participation, Profit-Sharing, Worker-Ownership and Efficiency in Italian Producer Cooperatives', *Economica*, 52, (208) Nov. 449–65.

KAPLAN, R. (1984), 'Yesterday's Accounting Undermines Production', *Harvard Business Review*, 84, (4): 95–101.

KENDRICK, J. (1985), 'Measurement of Output and Productivity in the Service Sector', in R. Inman (ed.), *Managing the Service Economy: Prospects and Problems* (Cambridge).

KNEE, and WALTERS, D. (1987), *Retail Strategy* (London).

KRUSE, D. (1984), *Employee Ownership and Employee Attitudes: Two Case Studies* (Pennsylvania).

LASLETT, P. (1983), *The World We Have Lost: Further Explored* (London).

LEWIS, J. S. (1954), *Partnership For All* (London).

LONG, R. (1982), 'Worker Ownership and Job Attitudes: A Field Study', *Industrial Relations*, 21, (2): 196–215.

LUKES, S. (1973), *Individualism* (Oxford).

MACINTYRE, A. (1981), *After Virtue* (London).

MAGUIRE, P. (1988), 'Co-operation and Crisis: Government, Co-operation and Politics 1917–22', in S. Yeo (ed.), *New Views of Co-operation* (London).

MARRIS, R. (1964), *The Economic Theory of 'Managerial Capitalism'* (London).

MIRRLEES, J. A. (1976), 'The Optimal Structure of Incentives and Authority Within an Organisation', *Bell Journal of Economics*, 7: 105–31.

MORISHIMA, M. (1982), *Why Has Japan Succeeded?* (Cambridge).

MORSE, G. (1983), *Charlesworth and Cain's Company Law*, 12th edn. (London).

NELSON, R., and WINTER, S. (1982), *An Evolutionary Theory of Economic Change* (Cambridge, Mass.).

NICHOLSON, J. L. (1967), 'The Measurement of Quality Changes', *Economic Journal*, Sept. 152–530.

NOTEBOOM, B. (1980), *Retailing: Applied Analysis in the Theory of the Firm* (Uitthoorn).

—— (1982), 'A New Theory of Retailing Costs', *European Economic Review*, 17: 161–86.

NOZICK, R. (1974), *Anarchy, State and Utopia* (Oxford).

PARFIT, D. (1984), *Reasons and Persons* (Oxford).

PARSONS, T. (1949), *The Structure of Social Action* (Glencoe, NY).

—— (1956), 'Suggestions for a Sociological Approach to the Theory of Organisation', *Administrative Science Quarterly*, 1, (1): 63–85.

PASCALE, R., and ATHOS, A. (1981), *The Art of Japanese Management* (New York).

PEARSON, R., and PIKE, G. (1989), 'The Graduate Labour Market in the 1990s', Institute of Manpower Studies, University of Sussex, No. 167.

PETERS, T. (1987), *Thriving on Chaos* (London).

POOLE, M. (1989), *The Evolution of Economic Democracy: Profit Sharing and Employee Shareholding Schemes* (London).

PRAIS, S., and JARVIS, V. (1989), 'Two Nations of Shopkeepers: Training for Retailing in France and Britain', *National Institute Economic Review*, May.

PUTTERMAN, L. (1984), 'On Some Recent Explanations of Why Capital Hires Labour', *Economic Inquiry*, 22: 171–87.

RAJAN, A. (1987), *Services—The Second Industrial Revolution? Business and Jobs Outlook for the UK Growth Industries* (Guildford).

RAMSAY, H. (1977), 'Cycles of Control: Worker Participation in Socio-logical and Historical Perspective', *Sociology*, 11: 481–506.

—— (1983), 'Evolution or Cycle? Worker Participation in the 1970s and 1980s, in C. Crouch and F. A. Heller (eds.) *International Yearbook of Organisational Democracy*, vol. 1 (Chichester), 203–25.

RASMUSSEN, E. (forthcoming), 'Stock Banks and Mutual Banks', *Journal of Law and Economics* cited in Hansmann, H. 'Ownership of the Firm' *Journal of Law, Economics and Organisation*, 4, (2) (Fall 1988), 282n.

RAVENSCRAFT, D., and SCHERER, D. (1987), *Mergers, Sell-offs and Economic Efficiency* (Washington, DC).

REED, M. (1985), *Redirections in Organisational Theory* (London).

REES, R. (1985), 'The Theory of Principal and Agent Part One', *Bulletin of Economic Research*, 37, (1).

ROBERTSON, J. A. S., BRIGGS, J. M. and GOODCHILD, A. (1982),

'Structure and Employment Prospects of the Service Industries, Department of Employment Research Paper No. 30, July.

ROSEN, C. M., KLEIN, K. J., and YOUNG, K. M. (1986), *Employee Ownership in America* (Lexington, Mass.).

ROWTHORN, R., and WELLS, J. (1987), *Deindustrialisation and Foreign Trade* (Cambridge).

RUSSELL, P. (1938), *Power: A New Social Analysis* (London).

RYAN, A. (1984), *Property and Political Theory* (Oxford).

SELZNICK, P. (1949), *TVA and the Grass Roots: A Study of Politics and Organization* (Berkeley, Calif.).

SINCLAIR, P. (1987), *Unemployment* (Oxford).

SISSON, K. (1989) (ed.), *Personnel Management in Britain* (Oxford).

SMITH, A. D. (1972), 'The Measurement and Interpretation of Services Output Changes', National Economic Development Office.

SMITH, G. R. (1986), 'Profit Sharing and Share Ownership in Britain', *Employment Gazette*, 94: 380–5.

SMITH, S. (1988), 'How Much Change at the Store? The Impact of New Technologies and Labour Processes on Managers and Staffs in Retail Distribution', in Knights, D. and Willmot, H. (eds.) *New Technology and the Labour Process* (London).

TAYLOR, C. (1985), *Human Agency and Language: Philosophical Papers I* (Cambridge).

TAYLOR, M. (1987), *The Possibility of Cooperation* (Cambridge).

TEW, B. (1959), 'Our Data and Methods of Analysis' in Tew and Henderson (eds.) (1959).

——, and HENDERSON, R. F. (1959), (eds.), *Studies in Company Finance: A Symposium on the Economic Analysis and Interpretation of British Company Accounts* (Cambridge).

THOMPSON, E. (1963), *The Making of the English Working Class* (London).

THOMPSON, J. D. (1967), *Organizations in Action: Social Sciences Bases of Administrative Theory* (New York).

THURIK, A. (1984), *Quantitative Analysis of Retail Productivity* (Delft).

THRULEY, K., and WOOD, S. (1983), 'Business Strategy and Industrial Relations Strategy', in Thurley, K. and Wood, S. (eds.) *Business Strategy and Industrial Relations Strategy* (Cambridge) 197–224.

TUCKER, K. A. (1975), *Economies of Scale in Retailing* (Farnborough).

—— (1978), *Concentration and Costs in Retailing* (Farnborough).

——, and YAMEY, B. S. (1973) (eds.), *Economics of Retailing: Selected Readings* (Harmondsworth).

UDO, P. (1986), *Corporate Paternalism and Part-Time Workers: The John Lewis Partnership and Marks and Spencer*, London School of Economics, Dept. of Industrial Relations.

VANEK, J. (1970), *The General Theory of Labor-Managed Market Economies* (Ithaca, NY).

VICKERS, J., and YARROW, G. (1987), *Privatisation: An Economic Analysis* (Oxford).

WADHWANI, S. (1988), *On the Efficiency of Financial Markets*, London School of Economics Financial Markets Group Special Paper Series No. 1.

WADHWANI, S., and WALL, M. (1988), 'The Effects of Profit-Sharing on Employment, Wages, Stock Returns and Productivity: Evidence from UK Micro-Data', London School of Economics Centre for Labour Economics Discussion Paper No. 311.

WARD, B. (1958), 'The Firm in Illyria: Market Syndicalism', *American Economic Review*, 68: 566–89.

WEITZMAN, M. (1984), *The Share Economy: Conquering Stagflation* (Cambridge, Mass.).

—— (1986), *The Case for Profit Sharing* (London).

—— (1987), 'Steady State Unemployment Under Profit Sharing', *Economic Journal*, 97: 86–105.

WHYTE, W. F., HAMMER, T., MEEK, C., NELSON, R., and STERN, R. (1983), *Worker Participation in Ownership* (Ithaca, NY).

WILLIAMS, R. (1985), *The Country and the City* (London).

WILLIAMSON, O. E. (1964), *The Economics of Discretionary Behaviour* (Englewood Cliffs, NJ).

—— (1981), 'The Modern Corporation: Origins, Evolution, Attributes', *Journal of Economic Literature*, 19, (4): 1537–68.

Index